Maurice Chauncy

The history of the Sufferings of Eighteen Carthusians in England

Maurice Chauncy

The history of the Sufferings of Eighteen Carthusians in England

ISBN/EAN: 9783743399839

Manufactured in Europe, USA, Canada, Australia, Japa

Cover: Foto ©ninafisch / pixelio.de

Manufactured and distributed by brebook publishing software
(www.brebook.com)

Maurice Chauncy

The history of the Sufferings of Eighteen Carthusians in England

CONTENTS.

INTRODUCTION.

WITH SOME ACCOUNT OF DOM MAURICE CHAUNCEY, THE AUTHOR
OF THIS HISTORY.

THE history of which a translation is here offered, was
written by Dom Maurice Chauncey, a monk of the London
Charter House about the year 1539, shortly after the des-
truction of that House by Cromwell and his agents. It
describes in simple and touching language the condition of
the House just before its downfall, which was then recent—
the measures adopted to force the new dogma of the Royal
Supremacy upon its members—the death and sufferings of
those who refused the oath, and the dispersion of the rest
after many and severe trials.

Dom Maurice Chauncey was born in Hertfordshire about
A.D. 1513. He was educated at Oxford and Gray's Inn, and
entered the Carthusian Order before he was twenty, and was
professed in 1534, Blessed John Houghton being then Prior.
During the persecution which followed that Martyr's death,
Dom Maurice was zealous in resisting the endeavours of
Cromwell to induce the monks to acknowledge the supremacy
of the King, and was one of four who were sent away from
the London House into another House of the Order near

Hull, with the object, it would seem, of breaking down his constancy. He returned after a time to London, and partly through the influence of the Monks of St. Bridgett at Sion House, and partly cajoled by representations and promises which gave him hopes that his taking the oath would preserve the London House—he yielded, and took the oath ; but speedily repented, and for ever afterwards deeply grieved over what he had done.

In 1538, the London House was broken up, and the monks expelled on a small pension, which, it seems probable, Dom Maurice never received, as he at once fled into Belgium, and was received, with one London Lay-brother, the companion of his flight, into the Carthusian House of Val de Grace, near Bruges, where he renewed his vows.

Sixteen years afterwards, in June, 1555, on the accession of Queen Mary, he returned into England, and with some others who had gone abroad, and some who had remained in England, he restored the Carthusian Observance at Sheen, in Surrey, at the old Carthusian House there, of which he became Prior. On the death of Queen Mary, the monks were again driven out of England, and were received into the Carthusian House of Val de Grace, and after two years, he was made Prior of that House, by the General Chapter. When, however, the numbers increased, he was permitted to choose a place where he and his fellow-countrymen could live by themselves, so he bought a house in Bruges, to which he gave the name of Sheen Anglorum.

Here he remained until 1578, when the Catholic Religion

in that region being overthrown, the monasteries also were broken up.

Dom Maurice and his companions fled into France without resources, seeking and not finding where they could be received. They settled at length at Louvain, in the greatest poverty. Dom Maurice, as Prior, then went to Spain to implore the King to help them, and having accomplished his mission, at once set out to return, but seized with illness on the journey, he took refuge in the Carthusian House in Paris, where he shortly afterwards died, on the 12th of July, 1581, aged sixty-eight years. On his body being prepared for burial, there was found fastened in it, an iron chain, the instrument alike and the witness of his lasting penance.

It remains to mention that by an ordinance of the General Chapter of the Sacred Carthusian Order, held at the Grande Chartreuse on the 9th of May, 1887, and following days, a feast of the Order, in commemoration of these martyrs, was appointed to be kept on the 4th of May, in accordance with the decree of the Congregation of Rites of the 29th of December of the previous year.

THE AUTHOR'S PREFACE.

To the Reverend Father, Dom John, Prior of the Grande Chartreuse, most worthy Primate of our whole Carthusian Order, Brother Maurice Chauncey, an Englishman, undeserving the name of Religious, offers most willing reverence and obedience.

IT having pleased Almighty God to give sleep and rest from their labours to the beloved Fathers and professed members of the House of our Carthusian Order near the city of London, formerly dedicated in honour of the Annunciation of the most Blessed Mother of God, the most sweet Virgin Mary; I have thought it would be worth while, Reverend Father, to make you better acquainted with their sufferings and death; for since that sacrilegious altar was set up in Bethel* whereby we were prevented from any longer going up to Jerusalem, or being converted to the Lord, none of our Congregation has reported to you any particulars of their death; for surrounded as we were with spies, we neither dared, nor were able to do so. But now, God having delivered me from the snare of the fowler,† and having

* 3 Kings xii. 32.   † Psalm cxxiii. 7.

removed me to a place of security, I have felt compelled
to acquaint your Reverend Paternity with all that happened
to us.   But in the first place,. following the example of the
children of Israel, who, arriving at the River Jordan, on their
journey into the Promised Land, thought it well to take
of the hardest stones from the bed of the river, and to set
them up in the camp, for a perpetual memorial to the
children of Israel of the way by which the Lord had brought
them out, the Ark of the Testament, meanwhile, remaining
in the midst of the stream,* until the completion of all those
things which the Lord had commanded Josue to do; in like
manner, I, to make it better known of what sort those men
were whom the Lord chose for His inheritance, to follow the
Lamb wheresoever He should go, in life or in death, before
I pass over our Jordan, being about to bring thence my
coffer full of the relics of the servants of God, I will interpose
some things which may not be out of place, in order to set
up with the hardest stones of our river (not, however, with
the intention of conveying any lesson, but rather for the
refreshment of the spirit), a place of rest for travellers
wearied by the long and tedious journey over this terrible
mountain, a place of horror and solitude; also, that I may
not seem to be beginning my narration at the point where
they ended their happy course; and more especially, because
Holy Scripture teaches, that a wise son is the glory of his
father, especially if the son does only what he sees the father
do, and what he has learnt from him.   For a father makes

* Josue iv. 1—10.

his truth and his virtue known to his sons. Wherefore, what I relate of a more excellent kind, whether of the Father, or of the sons, and the manner of living in that Convent, I do it, that God may be glorified as well in the father as in the sons. And let no one suppose that I relate these things from a desire of praise or human glory (because I was professed in that Convent), or that the good works done there should be seen of men. For I am altogether devoid of any claim to praise or glory. I rather deserve reproach and ignominy. Judas, the traitor, was numbered among the twelve Apostles ;* he heard, saw, and did as the rest, yet was reprobate. To begin a good work is nothing ; to finish it is deserving of honour ; so that when a man hath finished, then he begins to receive the crown of life that God hath promised to those who persevere to the end.† Satan was present among the sons of God, but is never praised ;‡ I indeed, went forth from these ; the thing is notorious : but I was not of them, for if I had been of them, I should have remained with them to drink of the chalice which they also drank. I, Saul among the Prophets, I, a son of Ephrem, drawing and loosing a bow, turned back in the day of battle, I drew back in not keeping what had been put in care. Such sanctity flourished among them that I am unworthy to be called or reckoned, and much less to be praised as one of them. If to me, ejected from their fellowship, but recounting things concerning these children of men, praise were thought due, much more should praise be ascribed

* Acts i. 17.   † St. James i. 12.   ‡ Job i. 6.

(but this were impious) to the fallen angel, proclaiming wonderful things concerning the Son of God,[*] when he said to the Lord Jesus, We know Thee, Who Thou art, Thou art the Son of God. Empty and vain, indeed, is that exaltation (if I may trust St. Chrysostom and my own little experience), which the testimony of conscience reproves. Let, therefore, no one call me Noemi,[†] or rather bitter, because the Lord hath afflicted me and filled me with bitterness. I went out full, and the Lord brought me back empty. Let it suffice to me, if, from my present needs, glory to the Highest resound to the Most High, and on earth veneration be paid to those Saints, by men of goodwill, and by the mercy of God, as I earnestly pray, the demolished vine of our holy Religion rise again, and spread its branches from sea to sea, and from the river to the ends of the earth.[‡] But I say not these things as if by accepting this mortification of empty glory, I should be perfect, but that the tongues of other men's praise being removed, I may more readily be freed from the fire of concupiscence which smoulders in my bones, so as by any means to stimulate my flesh to imitate the virtues of those of whom I presume to speak;[§] and may at length, by the grace of God and their merits, be re-ingrafted into my own olive-tree;[§] which that Thou wouldst be pleased speedily to grant, most sweet Jesus, I beseech Thee. Amen.

---

[*] Isaias xiv. 12.   [†] Ruth i. 20.
[‡] Psalm lxxix. 12.; lxxi. 8.   [§] Romans xi. 17.   [||] Romans xvi. 24.

CHAPTER FIRST.

IN order to advance more conveniently in this narrative, I begin by describing the venerable Father Prior of the same house. This Reverend Father, by name John Houghton, of whom I first speak, was born of honourable parents in the county of Essex. Leaving his parents for the study of letters, he progressed so well in them, that he obtained with credit the degree of Bachelor in both laws in the University of Cambridge. His parents then thought to induce him to marry, perceiving which, having no inclination for the conjugal state, and having resolved to dedicate himself to the service of God, he privately left them, and flying secretly, dwelt in concealment with a devout priest until he could take Sacred Orders, including the Priesthood. Having taken these, he returned to his parents, and at length induced them (even if unwillingly), to consent to all he desired; and so living laudably in the sacerdotal state for four years, he afterwards aspired to rise to higher things, as a stag in the morning.*

And in the twenty-eighth year and flower of his age, he began to trample under foot this perishing world, to accomplish which the more speedily, the more securely,

---

* He seems to allude to the Hebrew title of Psalm xxi., *Pro cervâ matutina.*

B

and with the utmost profit, inflamed with holy longing, he laboured with the whole bent of his soul to take on his weak shoulders the most religious and sweet yoke and observance of the Carthusian Rule, earnestly demanding in the said house of the Salutation of the most Blessed Virgin Mary, by humble and constant prayers, to be clothed in the holy habit of our Order. And when after long probation, he was clothed, putting off the old man he truly put on the new man, which after God is created, even our Lord Jesus Christ. For he led there for twenty years a very remarkable life, in much austerity, in humility, in patience, and perfect self-mortification, a diligent keeper of his cell and silence, always concealing and repressing the grace given him, lest it should be noticed, desiring always to be unknown and deemed worthy of no estimation

CHAPTER SECOND.

HOW HE WAS CHOSEN SACRISTAN IN THE HOUSE OF LONDON.

TRULY, as a city set on a hill cannot be hid, or the windows of a house so closely shut that the light within should not be somewhere visible from without, according to the verse:

> Quoque magis tegitur, tectus magis æstuat ignis,
> Sicut et caminius injectis exsilit aquis;
> Et flamma in sublime extollit comas.*

Not unlike this is the innate property and condition of grace and virtue, for the more it is concealed and repressed, lest it should be manifest, so much the more and the more quickly does it spring forth and increase; whilst the more freely it is enlarged and spread out in order to be seen, so much the more quickly does it turn to dust, vanish and come to nothing. "Glory follows him who flies from it," as was most fully illustrated in this holy Father. He chose to be abject in the house of the glorious Virgin Mother of God, and was accounted by men virtuous and holy. He desired to be despised, and honour followed and took hold of him, if honour it may be called, but to him and to all saints, such things bring more labour than honour, *plus oneris, quam honoris,* though the untameable colt of an ass may rejoice and be glad as much in this kind of sensuality as in true honour. But this

---

* The more restrained it is, the more the pent-in fire rages, and as fire in a furnace, on water being thrown on it, leaps up on high in lambent flame.

devout Father, having lived a long time in hidden sanctity, took, under obedience, the office of sacristan,* which, of all duties and obediences, was most pleasing to him, because it was his delight to be always in the church, and to be occupied day and night in ecclesiastical ministrations, and to be the servant of all his brethren; all which things he performed with great alacrity, industry, and reverence, availing himself of all occasions to advance and to merit by humility, lowliness, and labour.

During the time he was in this office, this thing occurred which is worthy of all remembrance. A certain devout Father, attacked by a pestilential disease, was near his end; who, when he had received the Body of our Lord, was unable, through extreme weakness, to swallow It, and at once cast It forth. The Father Vicar, in the absence of the Father Prior, gathered up the Sacred Host, together with all that had been cast forth, and took It to the cell of this holy Father, John Houghton, then sacristan, to be burnt. A fire having been lighted, these Fathers contended together which of them should cast It in—neither of them presuming to do this, It was reserved for two days. On the third day the devoted sacristan separated, as far as he could, the venerable Sacrament of the Body of Christ from the uncleanness with which It was mixed, and placed It in a chalice, intending to consume It on his next celebration. But previously he called to him a certain devout Lay-brother, to whom God had frequently revealed with certainty many things, as was known throughout the house (for whatever he asked of God, God immediately gave him an answer, so familiar was he and so pleasing

---

* "The sacristan, who ought to be truly religious, of mature age, and of grave character, receives a key from the Prior, and with the key, the custody of all the things that are in the church" (Stat. pt. I, cap. xxiii.).

and dear to God). To him, therefore, the Father Sacristan communicated his intention, requesting him in so difficult a matter to pray to God, to know His good pleasure, for he was afraid to burn It, and had some kind of horror in consuming it. The Lay-brother,* to fulfil the commands laid on him, earnestly besought the Divine clemency to deign to give him in this matter some indication, and behold at Matins, being in an ecstasy, he saw a great multitude, whom no man could number,† clothed in white, each carrying a lighted wax taper, enter the sacristy, in measured step, and proceed to the place where the Body of Jesus lay, and there adoring with the utmost reverence, opened the chest, which was closed, and having made here a brief delay, disappeared. But what in the meanwhile they did there, remained unknown to the Brother who saw these things. But the Brother having come to himself, asked the sacristan in the morning, whether in such a place he had deposited the aforesaid particles of the most holy Body of Christ, and on his answering yes, he at once understood what he had seen. The most devout Father Sacristan having heard this, putting aside all fear, both of death and nausea, prepared himself at once with all alacrity to celebrate Mass, during which he reverently and with affection received that which had been set aside ; but no one knows but he who received It, how glorious that chalice was to him. Truly inebriating It was, so far as those who stood by were able to perceive. He feared not death who received the Author of Life, nor sickness who swallowed Him Who heals all diseases, nor had he nausea from what had been cast forth, because he tasted in spirit how sweet the Lord is.‡

---

* An old tradition flourishes in our Order that this was Brother Taylor, of whom mention is twice made in the course of this history. † Apoc. vii. 9. ‡ Psalm xxxiii. 9.

CHAPTER THIRD.

HOW HE WAS CHOSEN PROCURATOR, AND AFTERWARDS PRIOR AND VISITOR.

HAVING then, to the good liking of all the brethren, laudably fulfilled the office of sacristan for a period of five years,* he was chosen for that of Procurator.† O, what grief assailed him, what abundant tears, what sighs he sent forth, what bodily distress overcame him, who thus altogether against his will, is constrained to leave his beloved solitude and silence! Lia,‡ with her uncomely countenance, pleased him not; he preferred his first love, seeing that what had been, was better for him than what was offered. He delighted in solitude, where the sweet whispering of his Beloved could reach him in secret.§ He longed for the embraces of Rachael, fearing to be torn from them by many cares. Nevertheless, by the help of God, Whose right arm encompassed him, he was wonderfully preserved in peace. Wherever he went, wherever he was, whether in noise or in solitude, in the streets or in his cell, he lived a recollected life, drinking in peace; peace, because he hoped in peace, was drawn away from it by no affairs, being wholly intent on God everywhere. Most

---

* He was then about forty.

† "For so we desire him to be called who after the example of Martha, whose office he undertakes, has to be solicitous and troubled about many things" (Stat. pt. II, cap. vi. s. I).

‡ Gen. xxix. 17.   § Cant. viii. 8.

certain is it, that leaving himself for God, he received a hundred-fold even in the present life.*

And thus bearing himself in this office for three years, carefully, earnestly, and piously, beloved alike by God and man, the Priorate of Beauvale† falling vacant, he was compelled to undertake and bear that burthen. Thither he migrated, but after ministering there for scarcely half a year, he was recalled to the house of his profession. For the venerable Father Prior‡ of the house of London, John Batmanson, had departed this life, in whose place this Reverend Father was chosen unanimously (as very rarely happened), and afterwards, in the second year of his priorate, he was appointed by the Reverend Father of the Chartreuse to be the principal Visitor of the English Province.

Thus, he who desired to be hidden and unknown, was by Divine Providence, to the edification of many, brought out into notice. It is difficult to describe in words, the things that he did in the course of his administrative labours, and still more respecting those that were hidden within him, for no one knows what passes in a man, but the spirit of man Inexhaustible, therefore, is the fount and torrent of glory of this our Father. But after the manner of my age, who am but a child, as well in years as in grace and manners, not knowing what to speak, yet now established in a fair meadow, going up and down in it, I will gather brighter flowers to make myself a garland, and would that I may do so, for the interior ornamentation of my own soul, by the fragrant imitation of my holy Fathers.

* St. Matt. xix. 29.

† Made Prior of Beauvale in 1530. We have no Abbots, not even in the Grande Chartreuse, whose Reverend Father styles himself "Humilem Cartusiæ Priorem."

‡ Chosen Prior of London. This venerable Father was elected in 1529, after the old man, Tynbygh, had been relieved from the office by the General Chapter of that year.

CHAPTER FOURTH.

OF THE PRIOR'S HOLY AND DISCREET GOVERNMENT IN HIS OFFICES, AND OF HIS VIRTUES.

THIS venerable Father was profoundly humble (which should be the end of every beginning), loving a companionable life with the brethren; for in his prelacy honours did not change his conduct, he remained always one and the same. He was never puffed up. If by chance any one called him "Lord," or gave him any title of distinction, he took it ill, and at once disclaimed it, saying it did not become a poor Carthusian monk to make broad his fringes, or to be called of men Rabbi.* When, however, any of the Brothers bowed to him, he received it as an occasion for great self-humiliation; nevertheless, he ordered them on no account to omit such-like reverences. On your account, he said, and for your sons, let it be done, lest our field should be uncultivated; our statutes recommend it, and the language of Holy Scripture not only permits, but enjoins it. He begged them, in observing such ceremonies, either towards himself or one another, not to be as serving to the eye, to please men, but in singleness of heart, fearing God, having God always before their eyes, doing all in His Name; and it is reported of him that in his daily prayers, he begged God, so far

* St. Matt. xxiii. 8.

as these prerogatives and reverences were exhibited to him
in virtue of his office, to be pleased to take and ascribe them
to the praise and glory of His most Holy Name, and to
supply by the conduct of others, his deficiency in love and
worship. Thus he always endeavoured to keep himself in
humility. When in another's cell with any of the brethren,
he behaved, not as Prior, but as a humble Brother, saying he
had left the priorate in his own cell. When, however, he
was in the cell which belonged to his office, or elsewhere in
the monastery, he bore himself as his office required, but
with the greatest modesty and humility. And the whole
monastery held him in such reverence, that they deemed they
could not exceed in manifesting towards him honour and
pre-eminence.

What shall I say of his patience? The injurious, reproachful, and contradictory words which he bore from apostates,
would, if they were related, suffice to prove it; but let them
pass. So patient was he, that on a certain occasion, he not
only did not resist one who rose against him, but falling at
his feet as a true solitary, gave his cheek to him that struck
him. He was filled with reproaches and smitten with blows,
until rescued from his persecutor by others. Nor even at
such a time did he reply with threatening or angry words,
nor did any one ever see him disturbed by any passion
of anger; and when he who had presumed to inflict such
things on the Father, was cast by the others into prison, he,
as a true follower of Jesus Christ, prayed them to spare him.
"Why do you strive so for my sake? What so bad has he
ever done to me? What evil hath he done to me? He
hath not hurt me. Why are you angry? This good Brother
was not in fault. It was the enemy of our souls who

endeavours to disturb our peace, and if I should be moved, he would rejoice who compelled this Brother to trouble me. Truly, my enemy shall not rejoice on my account. Therefore, release this our Brother; but as an example to others, let him be confined to his cell for some days;" preferring to overcome by lenity, than to correct by severity of justice. The cause being his own, it was a sign of great virtue to preserve and exhibit patience, and so he showed it; but in the cause of God or religion, if after a first or second correction, the guilty would not amend, then after the example of Moses and Phineas, and moved by zeal and the spirit of the Lord, making for them a scourge of ropes, he did not fail in severity.

Moreover, he strove with wonderful diligence to overcome, deny, and mortify himself, making this his chief study, whether he was within or without the cloister. This also was the sum of all his admonitions, in order that others might do the like. But what a warfare and what troubles he brought on himself in order to attain it, God knows. And although his principal endeavour was to conceal all things in which he was concerned, his wrestlings were not so hidden as not in some degree to be known to the men with whom he lived. For whoever saw him, well understood the internal conflict he carried on, not only against flesh and blood, but against the very prince of the infernal darkness;* in which, however (lest he should bring reproach upon his children by speaking), he always waited in silence for the salvation of God.† Nor did he ever complain to any of the burden or heat of the temptations; only to the Brother who lived in the cell which he first occupied, he sometimes said, "O Brother, if such and

* Ephes. vi. 12.   † Lament. iii. 26.

such a place could speak, they would tell you somewhat!"
What more need I say? To such perfection at length,
by the co-operation of Divine grace, did he attain, that the
virtues he had amassed, shone forth in him as in a most clear
mirror and book written within and without.

How great was his devotion, the daily flow of his tears
attested. For he had a peculiar gift of tears. Scarce a day
passed, in which his cheeks were not bedewed with them,
especially when celebrating Holy Mass, and sometimes even
in the refectory, so inebriated was he with a richness of
Divine love and devotion, as to be unable to contain himself,*—
and the tears breaking out, he left the table, and hastened to
his cell, which had so often witnessed his devout compunction,
and entering into it, he wept copiously, the more freely as the
more secretly, during the whole time of dinner.

Charity superabounded in him towards God and his
neighbour. If at any time he feared lest any germ of
bitterness might arise in the cloister, he quietly endeavoured
to root it out, before it had got to a head. He said not,
" Let them see to it, let them restrain themselves," but went
to them at once, and after carefully sifting the matter, he
checked by his monitions, mixed now with wine, now with
oil, the bellowing of the infernal beast, and the rising tumult.
And if any one was excited against himself, he was not
ashamed, in order to secure peace, to be the first to ask
pardon by humble submission. And nearly every month
openly in the Chapter, on his knees, and in tears, he asked
those present to forgive him all his defects, negligences, and
bad example, accusing himself in many things, in none of
which had he offended any one; but because "the just is first

* Gen. xiv. 1.

accuser of himself,"* he feared all his actions, knowing that
God spares not him who fails in his duty. Often he said,
" Bear, my dear Brothers, with some little of my folly,† and do
bear with me. I trust, in God, not to commit sin, humbling
myself that you may be exalted : I am become foolish for
your sakes, you compel me, I do it that you may be wise,
suffer me, and receive me as foolish." O height of humility
and perfect charity, never puffed up or seeking his own, that
he might profit others! What charity more perfect, what
humility more sublime! Truly had he learnt that Divine
saying, " The greater thou art, the more humble thyself in all
things ;"‡ and fulfilled that of the Apostle, " If any man
among you seem to be wise in this world, let him become a
fool, that he may be wise."§ What more foolish among men
than to be cast down and humiliated ? What wiser and
loftier than to be proud and lifted up ? But " the wisdom of
this world is foolishness with God, and what is lofty with man
is an abomination before God."‖ Wherefore, this holy Father
learned to glory in the folly of humiliation, and was made in
all things an example of good works.

To have and preserve peace and charity in the cloister,
was his highest aim ; and because he knew that austerity has
not its origin in good, he chose not to rule with austerity
and authority, but with the most unassuming moderation.
Towards young men who had been professed less than four
or five years, he behaved like Joseph to his brethren, showing
himself as a stranger,¶ speaking more severely and chiding,
lest by the abuse of lenity they might become bold. He
warned the instructors of novices to watch carefully lest

---

* Prov. xviii. 17.   † 2 Cor. xi. 1.   ‡ Eccles. iii. 20.
§ 1 Cor. iii. 18.   ‖ 1 Cor. iii. 9.   ¶ Gen. xlii. 7.

"they, as new plants in their youth "* should grow up in too much boldness, from which experience teaches many evils had arisen. With the elders, however, in order to relax stiffness, induced not through pride of birth, but by evil custom, self-will and want of self-mortification, through vain self-estima-tion, on account of long continuance in religion, he dealt earnestly, but gently and mildly, so as to make them pliant, and prepared for all things. When any one of the brethren, old or young, complained of anything as superfluous or fanciful, he checked him with moderation and mildness, reminding him of his vocation, and saying, "If you were in the world, good Brother, you ought not to follow your own inclination in all things, how much less here in the cloister. Do some violence to yourself against such hurtful suggestions, in order that with the violent you may acquire the Kingdom of Heaven."† He denied nothing to any with harshness, nor did he readily concede what they asked for, but he answered their applications with such mildness, that they departed happier on account of the self-denial imposed on them by his refusal, than they would have been had he granted their request. " The spirit of life was in the wheel of his words."‡ If any one of the brethren, in the pronuncia-tion and drawing out of words (according to the empty pomposity and fine-drawn manner of the moderns), ventured to read in an affected way, he earnestly and sternly reproved him, saying, "That such affectation was unsuitable to Carthusian simplicity, for the wish to seem learned springs from pride, though it yields neither erudition nor piety; therefore, I pray you, Brother, let the simplicity of the dove combined with charity, be our best science and learning, and

* Psalm cxliii. 2.   † St. Matt. xi. 12.   ‡ Ezech. i. 20.

let us follow the footprints of our Fathers, in sincerity before God and His Christ."

In regard to the Divine Offices and Services he was very vigilant, teaching always that uniformity should be observed in ceremonies, and all things, and that the chant in the church should be lengthened out, saying, "We come here to serve God, and to apply ourselves to His service. We are posted as watchmen on the walls of Jerusalem, by God the Judge of the living and the dead, never to cease from praising Him by day or by night.* Our Office is the same as that of the Holy Angels, who beginning before us, are united to all engaged in psalmody, and continue the praises of God when we cease. Let us, therefore, having such associates, do as they do, as far as our frailty permits. We could not be better occupied than with God. No exercise is more pleasing to Him or more useful to us. What can we do in our cells? Possibly all our time is not devoutly spent by all ; wherefore, let it not grieve us to be here. If we, who live on the patrimony of Christ and alms, and are very strictly bound to pray for all, hurry in God's service, or invent excuses for leaving the church, regarding as too long, the short and little time we are here, assuredly I know not how we shall excuse ourselves from injustice, in taking, retaining, and expending the alms of our benefactors and founders. How many of you feel wearied by gossiping with strangers, or about vain or useless things, even though you should spend the whole day in it, or how long would you not persevere in such things, without any tedium or unwillingness? And what about food, or drink, or sleep? When will you say of these : 'We have enough, or the time is too long? Let us hasten or finish.' St. Bernard thought all

---

* Isaias lxii. 6, 7.

time lost in which his body had to be refreshed with such necessary things. Another also, full of the Spirit of God, prayed the Lord to deliver him from these bodily necessities, in order that he might not so frequently be hindered by them from Divine contemplation. But in these days Jordan is turned backwards,* when many religious are mightily wearied when not occupied with vain and external consolations, for they do not regard the work of the Lord, nor consider the works of His hands. This, my Brothers, is not the monastic life, nor an aid to spiritual progress and edification, whereby our souls may partake of the Divine fulness; nay, is it even a sign of extreme heaviness which God will destroy; according to the Prophet, who says, ' Because they have not understood the works of the Lord, nor considered the work of His hand; Thou wilt destroy them and not build them up.'† For the people who knew not God, sat down to eat and drink and sleep. Not as this people should the priest be, and above all, the Carthusian, who has entered on a way of most excellent and perfect life, lest his punishment resemble theirs whose guilt he shares."

With these and many other like instructions, he exhorted them to lengthen out the chant in church. Sometimes during the Divine Office, he would go from his own place to the cantors, and admonish them to sing more slowly. If he heard them sing in a languid or low voice, he would say, he feared lest the love of God in their hearts was growing lukewarm, for as they sang languidly, so they loved God languidly, and God would on account of their lukewarmness cast them out of His mouth. He asked them also not to make distinction between days and seasons, at one time singing in

* Psalm cxiii. 3.   † Psalm xxvii. 5.

an undertone, at another loudly, for, said he, as there is no time appointed by our Heavenly Father, when we are to cease from His love, but are commanded always and at every moment with our whole strength to love Him ; so ought we never to desist from His praise, but to praise God always with our whole soul. Away with such laziness, let us beg and buy of God, gold tried in the fire,* and as the Angels in Heaven never cease from praise, never let weariness in His holy service creep on us unawares. Once also to their confusion (as he told them in their next Chapter), he left the church, when he heard them singing faintly. He was also always displeased, if any sang out of tune or a wrong note.

On a certain occasion, at Lauds on a Sunday, one side of the choir committed a mistake in singing the verse, *Dextera Domine fecit virtutem*,† therefore, in the morning, calling us into the Chapter, he said : "O dearest Brothers ! what did we do this night ? We went wrong in the psalmody of our God. Let us confess our faults. It is very wrong in us, who accompany the Office of the Angels, to commit such mistakes in the sight of God and the Angels. They never go wrong, and we do it through our negligence and carelessness. What we ought to do extremely well, we do with negligence. If, when we have done all, we are unprofitable servants,‡ of what sort are we in this our failure ? Let it not happen again. If, to an earthly king, one offers what is lame, weak, or tainted, will he not refuse it ? Will not such an offering give offence ? Cain was rejected, not because he failed to make his offering, but because he offered of his worst. His brother was chosen, offering of his best. What would earthly

* Apoc. iii. 18.   † Psalm cxvii. 16.   ‡ St. Luke xvii. 10.

lords say to their servants who behaved without attention in their ministrations? They require all things about them to be done with the greatest care and diligence; but we have been negligent in the service of our God, the ' King of Kings, and Lord of Lords.'* I fear they will rise up in judgment against us, and their well-performed works will condemn us for our carelessness and negligences, calling down on us with threatening voice that terrible Divine sentence: 'Cursed is he who doth the work of the Lord negligently;'† which the merciful Lord avert from us." And he straightway ordered them under obedience, that as they always had light throughout the entire singing of the Psalms, in all the Nocturns, and in Lauds or ferials, according to custom, so should they have them on Sundays; also that when any one sang alone, whatever it might be, he should have a light.

And because to him especially, all were confided, and from him would an account be demanded of the souls of each (the just to be admonished to persevere in goodness and justice, the unholy to return from his evil way, and the lukewarm to turn his thoughts to amendment), therefore, at least once a month he made it a rule to preach to the whole monastery, and with such sweetness of words were these his discourses filled, that where there was hidden fire "thick water"‡ was found, which flowed in abundance from the eyes of many; with which when their sacrifices were sprinkled, a great fire was again kindled, namely, greater devotion and new fervour. Nor did he speak in vain, for every one endeavoured to do as he taught. Such as he saw more fervent and quicker to run in the way of His commandments,§ these, on account of their defects, he sometimes more

---

* Apoc. xix. 16.   † Jerem. xlviii. 10.   ‡ 2 Mach. i. 20.   § Psalm cxviii. 32.

C

severely and openly rebuked, in order to preserve humility, and induce greater vigilance over themselves, and caution not to repeat such things ; also in order that through the growing fervour of the younger which there abounded, he might repel torpor in the lazy and weak ; for there were about twenty in that convent who had not attained thirty-eight years, but "who in a short space fulfilled a long time."* These he invited to the warfare of mortification, not only by word and example, but also exercised them in it, in very many ways ; at one time taking from them what they most loved, at another denying them what they most earnestly asked for, inclining them from one or the other, to learn to fight with their enemies, and timely to deny themselves, and with the greatest prudence he had regard to the character and disposition of each.   When, however, he proved any one in this manner, he again quickly visited him, lest he should be overcome by too much sadness, and this sometimes by himself, but more frequently by others, lest too much familiarity should breed contempt.   And then he sent them some little presents, considering that by such things the juvenile mutterings would be put to sleep, and also to encourage them to advance in the way they had begun ; for they were indeed children in malice, and quickly appeased, acknowledging that all had been done for their salvation and perfection.†   There was no murmuring or complaining there, because Father Prior had "done this or that," or "because he had thus treated me," but denying themselves, they made a virtue of necessity, and rejoiced to have both a cause and an occasion for merit and progress.   They themselves also sometimes begged him to put them to trial, by depriving them of such or such things, or otherwise.

* Wisdom iv. 13.   † 1 Cor. xiv. 20.

Besides these things, in order thoroughly to know the look of his flock, he inquired of each very frequently how they spent their time, to what spiritual exercises they were given, and how they were disposed internally, whether "they coveted their desire in the desert,"* or as spouses longed for the embraces of Divine love, or as servants thought over their former years in the bitterness of their souls,† and their progress in these things, whether, if at any time rust covered the most pure gold, and changed the splendour of its beauty,‡ whether, if they slept in the midst of the chosen ones, being as the wings of a dove covered with silver, and whose hinder parts were of the paleness of gold ; if any had lost his first love, then for a little space he would cease to speak with such, knowing that as a trial the beloved would either for a time turn aside or pass by, hiding his face in order to be the more eagerly sought after, but if the Brother delayed to return, and by bad example, by too much roaming about, or other frivolity, began to strike his fellow-servants, whereby it was evident the plague of leprosy would increase, he hastened to look after it ;§ nor did he give sleep to his eyes or rest to his eyelids, nor desist from holy warnings, sharp chidings, and pious entreaties, until that Brother had awakened his friend, and was again made whiter than snow by the operation of the Heavenly King, and had rebuilt the tabernacle that had fallen down, and found a place for the God of Jacob. The most devout Father was himself as burning flame or glowing iron, in the love of God, and desired that all about him should in like manner be ardently inflamed.

---

* Psalm cv. 14.   † Isaias xxxviii. 15.   ‡ Psalm lxvii. 14.
§ St. Matt. xxiv. 49.

He was, lastly, of great prudence, as was clearly shown by his doings in his own house, and in his visitations of other houses; so discreet was he in words, and so holy in works, that he was everywhere received as if he had been an angel of God, and all men wondered at his prudence and answers. When he was speaking, all placed their finger on their mouth and said, This truly is the servant of the Almighty. Our enemies thus judged, for the Lord Thomas Cromwell, a second Aman, the King's Vicar, whom the King had appointed over his household, and his whole kingdom, so that he was next to the King, and was the standard-bearer of all evil men; publicly, in our Chapter, before many by-standers, after the death of our Father, acknowledged him to have been a just and holy man. If he had held his peace, the stones would have cried out and proclaimed his holiness.*

He was kind to all, but to himself very strict and hard. Before he was appointed Procurator, he always kept the abstinence days† on bread and water. Afterwards, however, on account of his daily labours and fatigues, as well as visitations, as wherever he went, he kept all the fasts of the Order like the rest, being content with one fish. On common days of abstinence (as the custom was in that Province), and on high vigils and days of abstinence in Lent, he took only bread and drink, and when some of the Brothers urged him to have pity on himself by taking better sustenance, on account of his frequent infirmities, and the very great labours and sorrows which he bore every day, he said he was appointed a watchmen over them, and made a sign and

---

* St. Luke xix. 40.

† This does not mean abstinence from flesh meat, since that is perpetual, nor admits any exception, but certain fasting days which are called abstinence days in the Order.

spectacle to all ;* whose conversation, if it should seem dainty or too lax, would bring scandal on all, and boldness in evil doing.

Lastly, he was a great consoler of all who were tempted, or in trouble, because, having suffered and been tempted, he was better able to console those who were tempted. For he himself endured many and great temptations, but overcame in all, through, and for the sake of Him Whom he loved.

In prayer he was so frequent, devout, pure, and undisturbed, so impregnated with Divine love and spirituality, that the Father Vicar, the holy martyr, William Exmew, his confessor, told me frequently, that seldom or never did any particle of any of the affairs or other vanities with which he was engaged, after his election to the priorate, disturb his mind in time of prayer. At bed-time, after Matins, unless seriously ill, he never went to his cell, but rested upon any kind of bench, taking a log for a pillow, with a small cushion over it ; but he did not allow others to do this, unless they were strong in body, and practised in religious observance. However, he encouraged such to chastise their bodies discreetly, but forbade the young, for two or three years after their entrance into the Order, to act thus, on account of the many mischiefs that had thence arisen.

He ruled all with the greatest prudence, and sought in every way good things and peace to his people. He was slight of stature, elegant in appearance, shy in look, modest in manner, sweet in speech, chaste in body, and humble of heart. Amiable and beloved by all, most acceptable and dear to his monastery, all revered him, and there was none who would say of him a single bad word. He advanced and

* Jerem. vi. 17.

increased day by day, more and more outstripping his prior attainments, so that he was truly regarded by all as a great man. And men said of him, on account of his holiness and perfection, that he was worthy to be numbered among the Saints, even if he had died a natural death. What more? O ungrateful voice; what more? Many things, truly. But if I should speak with the tongues of men and angels, I could say nothing worthy of the virtues of this our holy and venerable Father. And what I have said, I call God and all His Holy Angels to witness, falls short of his merits. But now with grief and sighs, passing over, and leaving on one side many things about him, not for want of material, but on account of my inability, for I indeed too late bent myself down under his obedience,* and was too speedily deprived of his sweet and familiar friendship; I will introduce some other things concerning that our monastery, to fulfil the promise which makes known that two were one, not in one flesh, but in one spirit,† which makes both one, that one praise might be to both, to the Father and the sons together, both Father and sons being united, and ending in one and the same death.

From this it appears that Dom John Houghton had been Prior at least some months, when Dom Maurice Chauncey entered the Order. Dom John Houghton was elected Prior about the end of November, 1531.

† Ephes. ii. 14.

CHAPTER FIFTH.

OF THE PERFECTION OF REGULAR DISCIPLINE AND OF HOLY
CONVERSATION OBSERVED BY THE MONKS OF THE LONDON
HOUSE.

WHAT shall I say of the flock watched over by such and so
great a shepherd ? What else was to be expected, than that
they should hear the voice of the shepherd, and should follow
him ? No, indeed! no, me alone excepted, who like a lean
and scabby sheep, am cut off from the fold. If I should dilate
on the qualities of each in the monastery, time would fail me ;
but speaking generally, I say that that place was kept in
perfect peace ;* for it was built with stones hewn and made
ready, so that there was neither hammer nor axe, nor any
tool of iron, heard in that house of the Lord ; so refined was
it, that neither I nor those who were there long before me,
and knew the works of the Lord, and His wonders in the
deep,† ever heard as much as one reproachful word throughout the whole monastery (but in this survey I do not number
or include reprobates).‡ The highest and lowest were so
united in charity, bearing one another's burthens, that peace,
patience, longanimity, goodness, and charity, superabounded.
The elders did not roam about, but remained in their cells,
occupied with holy things—the restoration of the lapsed, the

---

* 3 Kings vi. 7.   † Psalm cvi. 24.
‡ See chapter 8, of "Reprobate Brothers."

reformation of the erring, and endeavouring to secure uniform observance throughout all the houses in the Province. And the young put on the glory and garments of war, to mortify their members upon the earth.* Behold the eight and forty strong men, the strongest in Israel, walking around the couch of Solomon, men of war, each with a sword on his thigh, because of the terrors of the night. Thirty monks and eighteen Lay-brothers (this incomplete number waits, I hope, for the year of the Jubilee), who bravely stood upon the watch over themselves day and night, aiming at virtue, each over himself. It was sweet to witness their combat and fervour.

Silence and solitude were there most strictly observed, so that if any one's father or near relation accosted him in the corridor of the cloister, going or returning from the church, or elsewhere outside his cell, although he might have leave, he did not answer, but made him a sign inviting him to go to his cell, if he wished to speak with him. Silence was nowhere banished, nor could they speak to one another without license. Previously to the outburst of these tempests, they never left the enclosure, not even the Lay-brothers. Throughout the entire day, except when going to or from the place of meeting, the cloister seemed as if no one dwelt there, unless some secular persons chanced to come on business. The utmost guard was kept of the eyes—they recognized none in the cloister, whoever he might be, but bowing, passed him, and the same in the church. They paid great attention to purity of heart and internal devotion, which are much impeded by such distractions. Tears were frequently in the eyes of many, and of some almost always, on account of which they were

* 1 Mach. xiv. 9.

unable, in the refectory or in the church, to read the Lessons, or to assist in the singing; in fact, some of them injured their sight by weeping. Their pious emulations were not as to who should be Vicar or Procurator (that they left to the Father Prior), or who should be greatest in the Kingdom of Heaven, (that they left to God), but which should most nearly attain to genuine mortification, deny himself most bravely, be most humble, most sincerely serve God, most fervently love God, most strictly observe silence, most heedfully keep his cell, most rarely have to confess faults in Chapter, come first into church, most willingly remain there longest, most lovingly devote himself to virtuous works, exceed in the greatest degree his obligatory works, and best observe the statutes and ceremonies of the Order. And this they attributed to the grace of God, and their own industry through Jesus Christ; in the performance of which things they watched day and night, animating and assisting one another to fulfil them.

There was there one heart and one soul in all things, according to the wish of the Reverend Father, who often said, "You load me, my Brothers, with a great burden, agreeing with me in all things. Let it be not as I wish, but as you wish." For all things were in common, *meum* and *tuum* were excluded from the cloister, so that no one had anything of his own, either in books or other things, but according to the request and good pleasure of all, they retained indifferently what each had in his cell. They greatly disliked what was fanciful, and loved what was mean, scanty, and poor. This, truly, was a mark of great grace and virtue, for nearly all in that monastery, as well monks as Lay-brothers, had possessed much wealth and estates, to which they were entitled by hereditary right, counting them as dung that they might win Christ,* leading a poor life. "Necessity" had no voice or place in the Paradise of my God, for it disturbs and causes sedition wherever it comes. For under the shadow of necessity, sensuality and self-will lie hid as a lion in his den,† to the ruin of souls, to whose expulsion even what was necessary, was driven out under the terrible watchfulness of the Father Prior; so that only what he considered necessary was so accounted. Necessity alone had place amongst them. Of things that were necessary, except of books, they had duplicates only, namely, of their habit, tunics, shoes, hair-shirts, and such-like. They were not tipplers, or given to much wine :‡ ordinarily, they had wine only twice a week, whether there was a feast of the Chapter or not, except in the principal weeks,§ and this in small quantity, namely, half a pint of wine and not more at any time. Remembering what cold and nakedness the Saints of God endured, who wandered about in sheeps' skins and goats' skins, some only made fires, and then only, when the cold was extreme. Also, even if the Father Prior had given them leave for a fire, they gave up their portion of wood, as alms to the poor. Nothing was done there without leave ; nor did any one dare to give or receive anything, however trifling, nor to drink or eat fruit after meals, except in extreme necessity.

In conferences or private meetings, one rarely heard an idle word, or a word about worldly affairs. If any one mooted such inconsiderately, he was admonished by his hearer, and thus the mind of the speaker was converted. Seculars often withdrew from their cells in tears, saying,

"Truly God is in this place."* For the Brothers were accustomed, on the first arrival of any visitor, and on receiving the salutation of seculars, to request them not to acquaint them with any rumours, or with what was going on in the world, but if the remark was edifying, they would ponder it in their mind, in order to imitate it, that it might not be lost to posterity; following the example of Hugh, Bishop of Lincoln, a predecessor of our most holy Father, who having visited some house of our Order,† on returning into England, after edifying the venerable Fathers of the Grande Chartreuse (as appears in our Life of him), having been asked by one of the Brothers, in ordinary conversation, about certain news, answered, "Oh, Father, to hear and relate rumours, though allowable for Bishops, is not so for monks. Rumours should not enter the cells or cloister; it is not allowable to leave cities and bring rumours into solitudes." This resounding voice sounded in the ears of our Brothers, indicating how grave a matter to them was the admittance of seculars. If the final tempest had not broken in upon us, such ingress of seculars into our enclosure would have been prevented as much as possible.

Truly, the length, sweetness, and modulation of the singing, stimulated the hearers to devotion and copious floods of tears. It was commonly said, If you would hear the service of the Church devoutly celebrated, go to the Charter-house. There were to be found ambassadors of other nations, there the tribes, the tribes of the Lord went up, old men with young, to confess the Name of the Lord.‡ Vigils with them

---

* Gen. xxviii. 16.
† He was first Prior of the house of Witham, then Bishop; died A.D. 1200.
‡ Psalm cxxi. 4.

every night, from the feast of All Saints to Easter, lasted at least five hours.* On ferial days, even on Chapter days, they rose at ten, but on the feasts of Candles† before ten, remaining in the church after three o'clock, and sometimes till half past three. From Easter to the feast of All Saints, on ferials, at eleven. And in order that they might be without solicitude, and might occupy themselves quietly with God, they purposed to supplicate the King to accept all their estates and possessions, giving them the annual rent of them, that they might be involved in no secular business. They kept the statutes according to the strictest interpretation, not failing knowingly in a single iota. And the venerable Father Prior with his Vicar, insisted that the monastery should be ruled in all things according to the traditional interpretation of the statutes.

* But here it is to be noted that during the singing of Nocturns, there was a brief interval, during which they could remain in the choir, standing or sitting.

† The feast of Candles is a solemn feast on which four candles or wax tapers are lighted, at both Vespers, Matins, and Lauds, whence it is called the feast of Candles.

CHAPTER SIXTH.

OF THE UNIFORM OBSERVANCE OF SACRED ORDER AND OF THE
RELIGIOUS CEREMONIES.

WHAT shall I say of the uniform order throughout the monastery? The Queen of Saba, among other examples, witnessing the order of the ministers of Solomon, had no longer any spirit in her.* Certainly, whoever might have seen the companies of those who ministered in this house of the Lord, would have been inflamed in spirit to serve the living God. For it was not as in the days of the Judges,† when every one did what seemed right in his own eyes; with us was uniformity of practice and ceremonies, without any distinction or variation. For the way was straight and clearly expressed in writing, so that fools could not err therein. Such order and harmony embellish Religion, and where order does not exist, there assuredly is dryness of devotion, perpetual trouble of mind, the utmost confusion of words, and discredit of Holy Religions; no concern for the affliction of Joseph,‡ and no care how God is served. Such disordered Religious serve only their own belly in eating, drinking, and sleeping. The inheritance of the Lord is not a speckled bird;§ in the sacrifices of God under the Old Law, the vestments of the ministers were not woven with threads of divers colours. The

* 3 Kings x. 5.   † Judges xvii. 6.   ‡ Amos vi. 6.   § Jerem. xii. 9.

Psalmist, moreover, says : " God in His holy place, God Who maketh men of one mind dwell in a house."* Wherefore, the Prefects and Prepositors of that our House, kept diligent watch that one and the same order should be observed by all, and in all things, that they should omit no ceremonies, but should observe them in all things, as strictly as the Statutes ; remembering that the Lord was in nothing more angry with the people of Israel than for transgressing ceremonies.† And he who despises small things, ceremonies and such-like, will fall by little and little into contempt of greater. For he who is unjust and unfaithful in a little, will certainly be so in greater if it be allowed. To avoid which, this saying was frequently inculcated by the voice of the preacher, " Keep My ceremonies, saith the Lord."‡ Also that all things should be done decently, fitly, and minutely, with maturity, gravity, and becomingness, and according to the uniform tradition and usage of our sacred Order.

* Psalm lxvii. 7.   † 2 Esdras i. 8.   ‡ 4 Kings xvii. 13.

CHAPTER SEVENTH.

OF THE WONDERFUL PERFECTION AND SIMPLICITY OF THE LAY-
BROTHERS, AND OF THE SINGULAR SANCTITY OF SOME OF THE
FATHERS.

AMONG the Lay-brothers, the same were in all things commanded and most religiously observed. For they were true
and entire Converts, in name and reality, from the world to
God. Most obedient sons, most dear brothers, most indus-
trious servants, most loving fathers, having the greatest
solicitude for the monks, bringing them no little consolation
in their afflictions, and most familiar friends of God, to whom
the Son of God often revealed things which He heard from
His adorable Father. For being very simple and illiterate,
they became possessed of wonderful ideas from what was
read, and from what they heard in the church and refectory;
and emitted brilliant sparks of spiritual knowledge to those
who questioned them. They resorted to and took delight in
spiritual exercises, and rivalled the monks in their study of
strict poverty and hatred of superfluity, the bare use of what
was necessary, forgetfulness of temporal and longing after
eternal things, humility and contrition of heart, shared by all
in common, self-contempt, and preference of others. They
were so equally imbued with holy devotion and fervour of
spirit, that two of them lying prostrate on the ground in time

of prayer, were elevated in the body from the earth at the same moment. The name of one was Roger, the other, John. In confirmation of this I will relate another thing, not less wonderful, for the edification of the Body of Christ.*

There was in our house in London a certain venerable Father, of unspeakable holiness, who had been professed over sixty years, during thirty of which, he had most worthily filled the office of Prior in that house, by name William Tynbygh, an Irishman. Before taking the habit of the Order, he went to the holy city of Jerusalem, where he was taken prisoner by the Haggarenes, and cast into prison to be put to death. Being in this strait, the day before he was to have been killed, he called to mind a picture of St. Catherine, which hung in the chapel of his father's house, in his own country. Turning to this picture with great fervour, he besought with frequent tears and sighs, the aforesaid Spouse of Christ for his deliverance. And persevering for a long time in this prayer, sleep fell on him, on awaking from which, he found himself sitting in the very chapel in his father's house, before the picture, having been miraculously trans-lated by the power of Almighty God (to Whom nothing is impossible),† over an immense space of sea and land. Wherefore, he and all who were present, greatly astonished, rejoiced at his unexpected arrival. Having thus experi-enced the Divine clemency, and the patronage of the most blessed Catherine, he related to the rest the thing as it took place. On hearing which, they began to hold him as a saint. Turning this in his mind, he fled secretly, and came to London, and shortly afterwards took the habit of our Religion in our house. In which, as another Anthony, he

---

* Ephes. iv. 12.   † St. Luke xviii. 27.

was exercised in the endurance and victory over temptations, in conflict with demons, and in holiness of life. For as the demon persecuted St. Anthony, so also they persecuted him, leaving him half dead. He indeed concealed all things as much as he could, in order to preserve humility; but on a certain night he was wounded by so many and such grievous blows, that he was unable to move from the place where he lay; or to cover himself with his garments; and was for these reasons compelled to be absent at the beginning of Matins. Being sought for by the Infirmarian, he was found lying on the ground, his wounds bleeding, and all things in his cell tossed about and in confusion; also in many other ways they tormented him. This holy Father was of such sanctity, that for many years before his death, he could never or rarely say the most holy Gospel, " In the beginning was the Word," without ecstasy and rapture. Once on a time, he was taken up into Heaven, where he was allowed to hear unspeakable words, and to see there and recognize many who had been his friends. His pre-eminent sanctity was admitted by all without any doubt. He died about the year 1531.

There were many others in that our Congregation replenished with wonderful sweetness of Divine love, and endowed with unspeakable holiness. Seculars said that if men on earth could possibly be likened to angels, and attain their purity, there were such in that House of ours. The venerable Father Prior often said, that he had angels under his obedience. I, however, said they were gods, and the sons of the Most High.* As regards the secret disciplines that many of them took, and the temptations they endured, in which the devil appeared to them in terrible forms, what

* Psalm lxxxi. 6.

D

annoyances he brought on them, with what bodily blows he afflicted and fell on them, and what sport he made of them, such and many more, rather to be wondered at, and more easily venerated than imitated, I omit to write, lest it should seem to be flattery, or boasting, or personal gratification, and not the testimony of truth.

Yet this is known to the whole house of Israel for truth, that God, wonderful in His ways, was pleased to work many wonderful and great things regarding His chosen ones living in that House. Tongue cannot say, nor the pen express, the great things God did by them; how many who were tempted were assisted by their prayers and holy counsels; how many who were afflicted and sorrowful were consoled, how many raised and rescued from the depth of despair; none left them unconsoled, nor did any perish who implored their help, submitting themselves at any time to their prayers; but were healed of whatever spiritual infirmity held them in bondage; when others not thus specially upheld, either stabbed, or strangled, or hanged, or drowned themselves. The high hills are a refuge for the harts,* the rock for the irchins, and what remains and was the greatest, God Who is before all ages, humbled them. Nothing was done through contention or vainglory, but in humility, each thinking the others better than himself,† they considered not their own things, but those of others, each gathering bunches of myrrh from the other's virtues, with which to build up humility in themselves.

And though I might discourse of the humility of each, I have not sufficient strength to do so, and I should extend my description too far, if I should attempt to make known all I

---

* Psalm ciii. 18.   † Philipp. ii. 3.

saw and heard, but I will not be silent about one who thought most humbly of himself, namely, Father William Exmew, who though a youth of twenty-eight, of very good family, very clever, and well versed in Greek and Latin literature, very zealous for religion, and a devout worshipper of God, without an equal in any House of our Province; at first Vicar and afterwards Procurator of our House, yet every night when at the end of the Second Nocturn he retired from the church (the statutes permitting him to do so), he withdrew in such confusion (as he often told me), as if he were reprobate from the Lord, deeming himself unworthy, not only to be numbered among, but to approach or remain in the company of the brethren when he stood up with them to praise God, and he said, therefore, he feared that he was chosen to the office of Judas, and in the end would be condemned with him.   All in the House knew with what tears he undertook the office of Procurator, and by what means he endeavoured to escape it. Never saw I any more heartily grieved and more bitterly deploring than when, having left the solitude of his cell, he went out into the bustle of secular life, being under obedience to undertake the office; when from a pelican of the wilderness * he became a fat bull fit for slaughter, from a night bird in the house, a bird of prey in the waters, and from a solitary sparrow became an eagle over the house of the Lord.   An immense grief then afflicted his humble heart, for he feared to lose the precious pearl he had found,† and having tasted the spiritual sweetness and quiet of solitude, he had lost all taste for the flesh and servile liberty.

Many others were like him in this respect, who would rather have sat in a corner of the house-top, than with a

* Psalm ci. 7, 8.   † St. Matt. xiii 46.

brawling woman in a house.* They showed their mutual charity, not only by word and deed in daily life, but more especially by that pious solicitude, which they bore for one another in all the evils with which they were encompassed, principally when persons set over them took away their provisions of food. How each for each compassionated the fasting and hunger of others, how they mutually consoled one another, and what expedients they adopted to succour and relieve each other's hunger and thirst. Their pious care for those who were in prison, as well within as without the house, likewise proved it; and in all these things it was manifest that they were true disciples of our Lord Jesus Christ. I make no mention of chastity, because nothing tainted or unclean entered that city.† What more? They went as the oxen in the way that leads straight to Bethsames, all in the same path, following each other, going and lowing as they went, lamenting the prolongation and the miseries of their pilgrimage, turning not aside either to the right hand or to the left.

* Prov. xxi. 9.   † 2 Par. xxiii. 19.

CHAPTER EIGHTH.

OF THE REPROBATE BROTHERS ASSOCIATED WITH THE GOOD,
AND THEIR TERRIBLE PUNISHMENT.

BUT if some, perhaps, were refractory, God would have made
a new thing on the earth, if in so large a monastery the
enemy had not sown tares, and if evil had not been mixed
with the good, for the trial of the good (for as there were
there many good, very good; so were there some bad, very
bad); and as the most merciful God ceased not to try the
good, as gold passes through fire, for their profit, by the
increase of merits and greater grace, that they might walk
from virtue to virtue; so also He tried those bad ones with
many callings and divers corrections, to make known to them
how great a crime it is to go back after having made a vow;
how much a foolish and faithless promise displeases Him,
and how cursed is he who sacrifices to the Lord what is weak
or lame;* and how much better it is not to vow than not to
perform. Having, at length, no further means of punishing
those who added fault to fault, He let them go according to
the desires of their hearts, which, of all punishments on
sinners, is the greatest and the most terrible sign of eternal
reprobation.† And He permitted them to fall (the natural
consequence of their sins), from good to bad, from bad to

* Eccles. v. 4. † Psalm xxx. 13.

worse, and from worse into the greatest darkness and blindness of mind ; because they accepted not the correction, but
called good evil, and evil good, all the days of their life.*   If,
therefore, as I began by saying, any one, or some of them,
was, perhaps, refractory, the Prior first of all corrected them
paternally, with a view to their amendment, not willing that
they should perish, but be brought to penance.   But when in
that cloister there was in any one an evil heart of unbelief,†
of departing from the living God, or any sinners who pro-
voked God, the most merciful Lord did not withhold His mercy
in His anger, to seek them out according to the multitude
of His wrath, but reserved all for the future ; ‡ but when the
sin was public, it was immediately and openly punished ;
of which punishments, which our Fathers have related to
us, I am not now to speak in detail.   Some, however, which
I, and the Lay-brother who is with me saw, I will relate as a
caution to others.   Happy is he whom other men's perils
make cautious.   The just also shall wash his hands in the
blood of the sinner,§ fearing and avoiding to commit such
things as he sees another punished for.   The wicked being
scourged, the fool will be the wiser. ‖

There was then, in that our Congregation, a monk named
Thomas Salter, much given to pointing out and defaming the
Brothers, even to seculars, who, nevertheless, never corrected
the evil that was in himself.   This man, after frequent back-
slidings, when on a certain occasion he was shut up in prison
in charge of a Lay-brother, that he might not again take to
flight—the demons, on a certain night, so terribly assaulted
him, and used him so frightfully that, unless his guard—who

* Isaias v. 20.   † Hebrews iii. 12.
‡ Psalm x. 4.   § Psalm lvii. 11.   ‖ Prov. xix. 26.

saw this in spirit, and stricken with exceeding bodily fear, perceived the demons entering to the apostate and vexing him, and who also heard the afflicted man's cries—unless, I say, this guard, by his devout acclamations and holy prayers, had quickly aroused him, they would have strangled and killed him, as the apostate afterwards related; who, after considerable delay, the demons having then departed, was hardly able to come to himself. There was another Brother, George by name. This man, vehemently longing after the flesh-pots of Egypt,* regarded all things belonging to the Order and to holy Religion as burthensome. Being once on a time at Vespers, wearied with the Divine Service, he left the church according to usage, and walked to the chapter-house. On entering which, the figure of our Lord on the Cross, which hung in sight of persons entering, was seen to turn its back to him on the Cross, averting itself wholly away from him, on sight of which he instantly became insane, and fell into desperation, and remained in that miserable state half a year. Afterwards, however, by the prayers of the Brothers, he was restored to his former health, which, nevertheless, was not accompanied by any amendment of life; for he fell into such a state of irreligiousness, that the convent was obliged to expel him from the Order, with license of the General Chapter. There was also another priest, named Nicholas Rawlins, a man of very tepid conversation, to whom it was trouble enough to remain in the Church, and who meditated apostacy. He, coming in on one occasion at Vespers, was so struck with blindness that he was unable to enter the door of the church, or even to find it, although he had placed one foot on the threshold, but beating about,

* Exod. xvi. 3.

turned hither and thither, and being led back to his cell at once, received his sight. He was, therefore, unworthy to enter the church. The same man at another time, whilst saying Mass, was struck with such terror and trembling of body as to be unable to proceed, and was obliged to take off his vestments and leave off what he had begun. In like manner, another Brother named Henry, of like tepidity and conversation, meditating the same things and not judging rightly, having to say the conventual Mass, was struck in the same manner with a horrible trembling, and ran from the altar into the sacristy, to take off his vestments as he did. And now I have begun to speak, I will add a fifth, who was also a monk in our house, named John Darley, who was exceedingly oppressed with many temptations. On a certain day, he complained that his nourishment was insufficient, and that the food given him at dinner pleased neither his eyes nor his appetite, saying, besides other things, that he would rather eat toads than such kinds of fish. Wonderful thing; the just God defrauded him not of his desire.* but brought him such a quantity of toads, that heaped up one on another, they covered the floor of his cell, crawling and leaping after him, wherever he went in his cell. They were his messmates at table, even leaping into his plate; they were also his bed-fellows. If he threw one into the fire, it at once leaped out unhurt. If he killed them, others came in their place, and the multitude daily increased, and continued with him in his cell for a whole month, nor could he in any way get rid of them. Having taken one with the tongs, intending to throw it into the fire, such a smell came from it as obliged him to desist; others also, at a distance in the cloister, perceived

* Psalm lxxvii. 30.

the smell. The toads remained in his garden for the space of three months. The Brother himself used very often to relate this, with great grief of heart.

So by these and other means, God discovered dark things;* He would not that so holy a brotherhood should be disgraced by such wicked deeds and enormous sins. For the sake of others, God permitted those to suffer such things, lest any should fall into the same example of incredulity and sin ; and for their own sakes, that being thus chastised they should desist thenceforth from such folly and wickedness. But such as were not converted, but made void their compact with God and His Saints, casting off the religious habit, went out from us with the license of the King. But enough has been said of such, and would that I could speak of amendment and penance corresponding to their sins and obstinacy, that the hope of those who are perishing might be the recovery of the lost. Now their evil deeds only are mentioned, that the ruin of those who go before may be a warning to those who follow.

But now to carry on the history I have begun, I will return to where I left off, having given examples both of good and bad, that where the examples of the good do not stimulate us, the misfortunes of the others may at least frighten us. For God is the same, His hand is not shortened, but is still stretched out to save and to punish. And I will return to my house, whence I went out; where that I may praise the Lord in His good things, may He be pleased to rebuild in it His tabernacle, and recall to it all in captivity and those of His who are dispersed, that we may be consoled in Jerusalem.† O House of the glorious Virgin, the most sweet Mother of God, formerly built with ramparts, now

* Psalm xxviii. 9. † Isaias lix. 1.

sitting in sadness, Mistress of the nations, thy name and
memory are in the desire of my soul!* In this dark night,
my soul hath desired thee, and my spirit within me likewise.†
From the morning I will watch unto thee, desiring to see thy
restoration. O, how blessed should I be, if there were
remnants of my seed to witness thy first brightness, which
thou hadst in the beginning. But wherefore these lamenta-
tions? Why is my soul drawn in with grief? Hast thou no
king, or has thy counsellor perished, that thy grief is renewed?
Has not God blessed thee, leading thee in the straight way
to the house of thy mother's brother‡ that thou mayest take
thence a wife for thy son Isaac.§ Is our God known only in
Judea? O burthensome consolation! my soul refuses to be
comforted in this manner. God hath indeed blessed me far
beyond my deserts or my desires, not regarding my miseries
and my faults, nor rewarding me according to my sins. But
if He were to take me up into Heaven, it would be a sign of
a degenerate mind and of too great ingratitude, nay, even of
the greatest impiety, to forget in this my old age my mother's
womb. And what shall I do? If I speak, my grief is not
silent, if I hold my peace, it leaves me not. I will, therefore,
be dumb, after His example, Who, when He was troubled,
did not speak.‖ Nevertheless, I will declare this truth and
lie not, my conscience bearing witness that my sorrow is
great and my grief overwhelming, not only for my absent
brethren, who desire from day to day, to see the day, for
whom an opening is not yet made in the mouth of Leviathan,
to enable them to pass this great sea without danger of

---

* Samuel i. 1.   † Isaias xxvi. 9.
‡ Dom Maurice calls the London House his mother, but the House of Val de Grace,
where he was received as a guest, the house of his mother's brother.
§ Gen. xxiv. 48.   ‖ Job xiv. 7.

death; but also for others, of whom I knew many, who would have believed through them, and been converted to the Lord our God, if a house of our Order should be rebuilt in that Province; but for myself not at all, except for my spiritual infirmities. And in order that I may be relieved in some measure from these through the mercy of God, I will embrace this Sunamitess with as much love and gratitude as I can,* not with such as I desire and ought, in the hope that she will let me partake of her good things, and will moderate the sorrow which has fallen on me through the death of my Mother,† and with her heat and fervour, warm again my flesh, grown cold by long continuance in evil days, when the pit was dug for the sinner:‡ most certainly knowing that here and in every tribe of Israel, great is the Name of the Lord. And although all those who enter the house of the Lord to pay the vows that their lips have pronounced, ought not to appear empty,§ but should approach their God in holocausts and oblations and the odour of virtues, with amendment of life and self-abnegation; nevertheless, our holy Fathers, in whose honour especially this history is written, offered for the adornment of the house of our God, besides oblations and voluntary vows, holocausts of their best, with the incense of rams and a feast of fat things. They offered oxen and goats, the skin with the flesh,‖ reserving nothing for themselves, neither body nor soul, neither outward nor inward, when, indeed, they contended for justice even unto death, a death of disgrace and horror, a death, moreover, of the gibbet, of sword and fire. Of which death we have now to speak.

---

* 3 Kings i. 2.   † Gen. xxiv. 67.
‡ Psalm xciii. 13.   § Exod. xxiii. 15.   ‖ Psalm lxv. 15.

But before I begin this (passing over the revelations with which the Lord frequently instructed his servants), I will say a few words of some remarkable portents.

———

CHAPTER NINTH.

OF THE PRODIGIES SEEN BEFORE THE MARTYRDOM OF THE BROTHERS, AND OF THEIR PREPARATION FOR DEATH; FIRST ON ACCOUNT OF THE SECOND MARRIAGE OF THE KING, AND AT LENGTH FINALLY ON ACCOUNT OF THE SCHISM.

IT happened in the year of the Lord 1533, which preceded that stormy tempest, a comet was seen in the air, extending its rays clearly and manifestly as far as our house. The whole Convent, retiring one night from Matins, saw and beheld the rays from that star flash and sparkle through a certain tall tree in our cemetery, and transfuse themselves and strike through upon our church and the place where the bells hung. Which was indeed a thing unheard of and unseen in past times. In the same year, our venerable Father Prior went out of the church after the Second Nocturn, and entering the cemetery, saw in the air a globe as of blood, of great size—and being terrified at the sight, fell to the ground in fear. Another Brother, on the same night, going into the garden of his cell, after Matins, saw the same, or a similar globe or sphere. Other things, not less extraordinary, occurred at that same perilous time, concerning two swarms of flies, one of which was black and extremely hideous, like the flies which are generated from dung. The others, of divers colours and oblong, like those that fly about in reeds over water. And those two swarms, infinitely numerous, rested at different times on our house and covered the whole of its surface. All which things we feared were the signs and forecasts of other events, and we all prayed to be converted to good. But in the following year what we feared came to us, and what we dreaded happened, and such great evils broke forth, by which, if God had not been merciful to us, all our past abundance might have been delivered over to oblivion.*

For, in the year 1534, when our city, the House, I mean, of the Salutation of the most Blessed Mother of God, the Virgin Mary, near London, was inhabited in all peace (for the laws were excellently kept, owing to the devotion of the aforesaid most religious Father John Houghton, the Prior, and to his piety and watchful care over his flock and the souls under his charge, who hated evil things), it happened that the enemy of the human race, envying their quiet, peace, charity, and holiness, stirred up the mind of the King of England to undertake some unlawful things in his kingdom, to which he willed to extort the consent of all his subjects, from sixteen years and upwards, as well Religious as secular. Of which evils the head or beginning was this, that all were required to consent to his second marriage, and to affirm it to be a good and lawful marriage, although his first wife and Queen was still alive. And when the Commissioners appointed for this business, began to carry out the edict of the King, and came to our holy Father to the intent that he and his convent should tender their consent to the King's ordinance, the Father replied, It was not his vocation, nor could nor ought

* Job iii. 25.

he or any of his interfere in Royal affairs; nor did it concern him whom the King was pleased to reject or accept as his wife, so long as he did not treat with him or his on things of this kind. But, not satisfied with this reply, they required that without any qualification, the convent being called together, should affirm on oath that the former marriage was illegal, and give assent and obedience to the second, and to the children begotten of it. Then when our venerable Father said, But he could not understand how a marriage celebrated according to the rites of the Church, and so long observed, could be made void, he was at once ordered to be imprisoned, with Father Humphrey, our Procurator, in the Tower of London, where they were detained for one month. After which, being persuaded by certain honest and learned men that this was not a legitimate cause on which to suffer death, they consented, *sub conditione*, to the Royal command, and being discharged, returned home, and were very joyfully received by us.

But when that oath was required of the convent, there was no little stir among them; which the Father perceiving, said, " My dearest Fathers, our hour is not yet come. For in that same night in which the Father Procurator and I were discharged from prison, I dreamt that I was not so quickly to escape, but that within a year I should be returned and received again into that same prison; and there I shall finish my course. There remains, therefore, as I think, though faith is not to be given to dreams, something else to be shortly proposed to us; nevertheless, let us live together without offence to God, as long we may." Whilst these things were thus under discussion, the King's Council, and the city authorities with their officers, came to take and conduct to prison the whole convent; for twice before they had returned empty-handed, having come to tender the oath. Then, on the advice and salutary exhortations of the holy Father, the Brothers, after consideration, resolved to acquiesce, and thus at length, on May 24, 1534, in the fourth year of the priorate of our Father, we swore as required by the King, *sub conditione tamen quatenus licitum esset*—"so far as it was lawful." We, therefore, being, as we hoped with a good conscience, freed from the belly of this savage whale,* began to rejoice with Jonah in the ivy on our dwellings, which sheltered and protected us from the rain, the storm, and the heat; hoping that we should rest securely under its shadow, without any greater tribulation. But it is better to trust in the Lord than in princes, in whom there is no safety.† For the Lord prepared a worm when the morning arose; which struck the ivy and withered it, leaving no trace of its former promise;‡ and this trouble made us understand the aforesaid prediction of our holy Father, and then we knew that a prophet was in our midst.

For, in the beginning of the year 1535, it was settled by the King, and enacted by the celebrated Act of his Parliament, that all should renounce the authority and obedience they owed to our lord the Pope, or any other superior in other countries, and should acknowledge under an oath, the King himself as Supreme Head of the Church, as well in spirituals as in temporals; under penalty of being held guilty of high treason, and punished with death. On this being promulgated through the whole kingdom, our venerable Father Prior convened the Chapter, and explained to us what things were impending.

* Jonas ii. 2.　　† Psalm cxlv. 2,　　‡ Jonas iv. 7.

Upon this there was great consternation ; and the Father said : " My sorrow is great, and my heart grieves for the young Brothers, who are numerous in this convent. For you see, my Brothers, how many young men are here, now living in innocency, on whose necks the yoke of burthen and the rod of a Master has never been laid ;* who, when once they shall mix in the world, may learn its works, and having begun in the spirit, may end in the flesh ; for evil conversations corrupt good manners. Associating with the wicked, they will soon be perverted. And it is as difficult to touch pitch, that is, the world, without contamination of flesh and spirit, as to pass unhurt through fire. Others of us there are from whose hearts, possibly, luxury is not entirely banished, to whom it would, we fear, in no slight degree, be dangerous to begin again to be involved in conversation with worldlings. What then shall I say, my brethren, or what shall I do, if I bring before the eternal Judgment nothing good regarding those whom God hath given me ?'

And there, then, was much weeping among them. Then they all cried with one mind and one voice : " Let us all die in our simplicity, and let Heaven and earth be our witness that we are unjustly destroyed from the earth."†

The Father sorrowfully answered, " Would it might be so, that one death may make us alive, whom one life hath brought to death, but I do not believe they intend so great a good for us, or to do themselves so much harm. Many of you are from a noble race. This rather, I think, they will do. They will deliver you elder ones and me to death, and. let the younger ones go where they will, into a land not their own. Wherefore, if my consent be alone required, I

* Isaias ix. 4.   † 1 Mach. ii. 7.

will throw myself on the mercy of God, and be anathema for these my least brethren,* and consent to the King's will, *si licite fieri possit*, in order to preserve them from so many and such great future dangers. If, however, they shall decree that all shall consent, and if the death of one (that the whole nation perish not), shall not suffice, then, may the will of God be done, and I would wish it might be by the equal sacrifice of all."

Oh, how was the spirit of this most holy man distressed, on this hand, his love of God not being willing to offend Him, on the other the dangers from which he desired to preserve others! What to choose he knew not,† yet the love of God prevailed,‡ mindful of His saying : "What does it profit a man to gain the whole world, but lose himself and cause his own ruin.§ Whoever shall be ashamed of Me and of My words, or that other, Whoever shall love any more than Me is not worthy of Me.‖

Nevertheless, this holy Father, thus straitened, added at that meeting, " Being ignorant, brethren, of what may happen, let us not be found unprepared. When the Lord shall knock at the gate, let us dispose ourselves as if we were immediately to die."

Then he exhorted them to prepare their hearts by a general confession to God, and gave leave that every one should choose any confessor in the convent whom he liked,

---

* Romans ix. 13.

† Observe what is said, "Not willing to offend God." From this he did not turn back, but sought how, without offending God, he could preserve his flock from peril—this (he being uncertain and hesitating), he revolved in his mind.

‡ Not finding any way to reconcile these difficulties, it remained that he should alone regard the honour of God, and so the love of God would prevail. Not that he hesitated between God and his neighbour. This is evident from, "What does it profit," &c.

§ St. Luke ix. 25.   ‖ St. Matt. x. 37.

E

and he gave to all power of plenary absolution,—and having
done this, on the following day he said : " Because in many
things we offend all, and every one is debtor to his brother,
and because without charity neither death nor life profit
anything, let us be reconciled to one another, and on the
third day, we will celebrate a Mass of the Holy Ghost, to
obtain this grace whereby we may fulfil His will and good
pleasure." When the first day had passed, our Father's
most salutary counsel having been followed and the day of
reconciliation being at hand, and our Father having made
a long and most devout sermon on charity, patience, and
firm adhesion to God in adversity, treating those first five
verses of the Psalm : " O God, Thou hast cast us off and
destroyed us,"* concluded his sermon thus : " It is better
for us to receive a short punishment here for sin, than to
be kept for eternal torments." Then he said : " My dearest
Fathers and Brothers, what you see me do, I beseech you
to do likewise." Then rising, he went towards the senior of
the house, sitting next to him, and kneeling before him,
humbly begged pardon and forgiveness for all his excesses
and sins at any time committed against him in thought, word,
or deed. And in the same manner the other did to him,
begging pardon for his. And so the Father, going first
through his choir and then to the other, made the same
request to each separately, down to the last Lay-brother,
weeping bitterly over each.† In like manner all followed
him one after another, each from each begging pardon. O
what grief was there, what profusion of tears ! Truly a voice
was heard in Rama, weeping and much lamentation ;‡ Rachel
weeping for her children, refusing to be comforted, fore-

---

* Psalm lix. 1.   † Genesis xlv. 15.   ‡ Jerem. xxxi. 15.

seeing the evils hanging over them. From this day any one who looked upon the countenance of our holy Father (which never before in any circumstances gave signs of change), knew how much he was suffering. For his face and changed colour declared the inward grief of his mind. There was over him a look of sadness and horror which showed to all the sorrow that had touched his heart.* The third day having come, in which the Mass of the Holy Ghost was to be celebrated in the convent, the devoted Father Prior prepared to perform it. During the Mass, it pleased the Almighty and merciful God to work wonderful and ineffable things.† It is good to hide the secret of a king, but honourable to reveal and proclaim the works of God; I will manifest the truth and will not conceal the hidden word. In that conventual Mass, after the Elevation, a whisper as of light air, faintly sounding outwardly to the senses, but operating much within, was observed and heard by many with their bodily ears, and felt and drawn in by all with the ears of their heart. At whose sweet modulation, the venerable Prior, overwhelmed with the fulness of the Divine illumination, and dissolved in tears, was unable for a long time to proceed with the Mass. The convent also stood in astonishment, hearing the voice and feeling its wonderful and sweet operation in the heart, not knowing whence it came or whither it went.‡ But all rejoiced in that most holy breathing, and well understood that God was indeed in that place, revealing to some His secrets, and dividing to each as He would. And as it is read in the Book of Numbers § (where the distribution of the Spirit to the seventy is described), that the Spirit rested also upon

---

* 2 Mach. iii. 16, 17.   † Tobias xii. 7.   ‡ St. John iii. 8.   § Numb. xi. 25, 26.

two others who had remained in the camp and had not gone out into the tabernacle, so also it happened with us; the Lay-brothers who were in chapels near the choir participated with wonderful sweetness, as well as the monks, in the grace poured out at the time of this Mass. Our holy Father in our next Chapter meeting made mention of this most holy Mass with much thanksgiving and devout exhortations to remain in the grace of God by instant prayer, by holy conversation rooted in humility and filial fear, and he added : " Not through me, but because of your holiness, hath God done these things." There was therefore a pious rivalry amongst them, who should think most humbly of himself; the Father attributed all to the devotion of the sons, these, however, to the holiness and merits of the Father.

What great constancy of prayer there was in that Congregation after that day, it is not possible for me to relate ; how with one mind they persevered in prayers, day and night,* and how they prostrated themselves before the High Altar after Matins asking help from the Holy One, that God would be pleased to protect them. How often did the holy Father repeat that prayer of David : " It is I who have sinned, these sheep what have they done ? Let Thy hand, I beseech Thee, be turned against me and my father's house ;"† and that other : " Holy Father, keep those in Thy name whom Thou hast given me."‡ I pass over many other sorrowful meetings and things that there took place.

While these things were taking place, the Father standing firmly as a bulwark for the house of Israel, and on the defensive to protect all those who had been committed to

---

* Acts i, 14.   † 2 Kings xxiv. 17.   ‡ St. John xvii. 11,

him, and neither yielding to threats nor blandishments, but waiting for the coming of the King's Council to give effect to his edict, the Reverend Father Robert Lawrence, Prior of the House of Beauvale, who had been professed in our House, came to London in order to inquire if all things were going well with our Father and his flock; for he was a very religious man and full of piety.* And it happened that within two days, the Reverend Father Augustine Webster, a professed monk of the House of Sheen, then being Prior of the House of the Visitation of the Most Blessed Mary, came also to London on business of his House; who, coming to lodge at our House, heard in what evils and dangers we were, and with what fury the King raged against us. For it had been told the King that the Prior and the convent of that House were preparing to resist him; on which account he was exceedingly angry.

* Genesis xxxvii. 14.

CHAPTER TENTH.

OF THE IMPRISONMENT AND TORTURE OF THE THREE PRIORS,
AND THEIR MARTRYDOM ON ACCOUNT OF THEIR CONFESSION
OF FAITH, AND OF THE CATHOLIC CHURCH.

THEN those three Reverend Father Priors, reflecting that
the anger of the King was as a messenger of death, resolved
together that they would endeavour to mitigate it (leaving
the result to the judgment of God), and would anticipate and
pre-occupy the time of the expected arrival of the King's
Councillors by going to the said Lord Cromwell, the King's
Vicar, to implore him to help them as far as he could to
get them exempted from the King's decree, or to obtain
some mitigation or relaxation from the tenour or rigour of
it, in regard to taking the oath.

Having then approached him and laid before him their
wishes and supplications, he not only denied their petition,
but ordered them to be sent to the Tower as rebels. Afterwards, at the end of a week's imprisonment, Cromwell with
many others of the King's Council came to them, and placed
before them the decree of the Parliament, which was, that
they were to renounce the authority of the Pope, and to
acknowledge that he had violently, falsely, and wrongfully
usurped his primary power, and were to repudiate all other
external powers, jurisdictions, and obediences, due or promised
to any person or order whatsoever; that they were to obey

the King and his officers only, and accept, believe, and affirm
that the King was supreme head of the Church, as well in
spirituals as in temporals. And when our Fathers answered
that they would consent in all things which and so far as
the Divine law allowed, he added : " I will admit of no
exception, whether it is allowed by the Divine law or not.
You shall affirm this entirely, fully, and in all sincerity of
heart, and take a public oath on it and firmly hold to it."
Our blessed Fathers replied that the Catholic Church had
always held and taught otherwise. Cromwell answered :
" I care not for the Church, will you consent or not ? " They
answered, that they having before their eyes the fear of
God did not dare to contravene or desert the Catholic
Church ; for St. Augustine had said that he would not have
believed the Gospel, unless the Holy Orthodox Church had
thus instructed and taught him. They were then again shut
up in prison.

On a day appointed they were brought before a court,
where being again questioned on this matter, they utterly
refused, saying that they would on no account or in the
slightest degree go contrary to the law of God or the doctrine
and practice of the Catholic Church. On this twelve men
were at once chosen according to law to deal with the matter
on oath, on this issue : whether these three men having
refused to acquiesce in and submit to the law made by the
Parliament were guilty of death or not ? This question having
been put to them, they deferred their verdict till the morrow,
for it was discussed among them for the whole day. All
opposed a verdict of guilty, and came to the conclusion that
our holy Fathers were innocent of transgressing the law,
and that they could not find them guilty of death. Mean-

while the King's Vicar, suspecting the good conscience of those twelve men, sent on the evening of the first day, before they had openly delivered their verdict, to inquire the cause of such delay and what they meant to do. In answer, they gave the messenger to understand, that they dared not to adjudge such holy men to die as malefactors, and he repeating those words to his master, the latter in a rage sent him back to them at once, to say: "If you do not find them guilty, you shall yourselves suffer death as transgressors." They, however, caring little for these threats, remained firm and at that time refused to consent. Cromwell hearing this, came to them quickly, and by his cruel threats compelled them to deliver their verdict, or rather their false finding in condemnation of our holy Fathers, and to find them guilty of high treason, which verdict being on the morrow delivered publicly, sentence of death was pronounced by the Judges in the form usual in cases of high treason; and so they were again cast into prison. After remaining there for five days suffering many inconveniences, but standing with great constancy against those who oppressed them,* the order for their execution arrived, which was in this manner (if manner it can be called, where beyond all human example, the barbarous cruelty of the worst tyrants was overpassed), namely, on being brought out of prison they were thrown down on a hurdle and fastened to it, lying at length on their backs, and so lying on the hurdle, they were dragged at the heels of horses through the city until they came to Tyburn; a place where, according to custom, criminals are executed, which is distant from the prison one league, or a French mile. Who can relate what grievous

* Wisdom v. 1.

things, what tortures they endured on that whole journey, when one while the road lay over rough and hard, at another through wet and muddy places, which exceedingly abounded.

On arrival at the place of execution our holy Father was the first loosed, and then the executioner, as the custom is, bent his knee before him, asking pardon for the cruel work he had to do. O good Jesu,

> Quis non fleret,
> Christi servum si videret,
> In tanto supplicie,
> Quis non posset contristari,

beholding the benignity of so holy a man, how gently and modestly he spoke to his executioner, how sweetly he embraced and kissed him, and how piously he prayed for him and for all the bystanders. Then on being ordered to mount the ladder to the gibbet, where he was to be hanged, he meekly obeyed. Then one of the King's Council, who stood there with many thousand people, who came together to witness the sight, asked him if he would submit to the King's command and the Act of Parliament, for if he would he should be pardoned. The holy Martyr of Christ answered: " I call Almighty God, and I beseech you all in the terrible Day of Judgment, to bear witness, that being here about to die, I publicly declare that not through any pertinacity, malice, or rebellious spirit, do I commit this disobedience and denial of the will of our lord the King, but solely through fear of God, lest I should offend His Supreme Majesty; because our holy mother the Church has decreed and determined otherwise, than your King with his Parliament have ordained; wherefore I am bound in conscience and am prepared, and am not confounded, to endure these and all other torments that

can be inflicted, rather than go against the doctrine of the
Church. Pray for me and have pity on my brethren, of
whom I am the unworthy Prior." And having said these
these things, he begged the executioner to wait until he had
finished his prayer, which was, *In te, Domine, speravi,** down
to, *in manus tuas*, inclusive. Then on a sign given the ladder
was turned, and so he was hanged. Then one of the by-
standers, before his holy soul left his body, cut the rope, and
so falling to the ground, he began for a little space to throb
and breathe. Then he was drawn to another adjoining
place, where his garments were violently torn off and he was
again extended naked on the hurdle, . . . during which our
most blessed Father, not only did not cry out on account
of the intolerable pain, but on the contrary, whilst they were
tearing out his heart, prayed continually and bore himself
most patiently, most meekly and tranquilly, so much so,
that not only the presiding officer, but all who saw these
things wondered. Being at his last gasp and nearly dis-
embowelled, he cried out with a most sweet voice : " Most
sweet Jesu, have mercy on me at this hour," and, as trust-
worthy men have reported, he said to the executioner, while
in the act of tearing out his heart : " Good Jesu! what will
you with my heart ? " and saying this, he expired. Lastly,
his head was cut off and his body divided into four parts.

In this manner, Reverend Father, is this your holy son
found faithful till death. He passed from this world to the
Lord, on the fourth day of May, 1535, in his forty-eighth
year, and the fifth year of his priorate,† like a good shepherd

---

* Psalm xxx. 2—6.

† Really, scarcely three and a half years, but our author reckons the end of 1531, in
which he was elected, and the beginning of 1535.

who gave his life, not only for his sheep, but for justice, and the faith of our Lord Jesus Christ.

Our holy Father having been thus put to death, the two other before-named venerable Fathers, Robert and Augustine, with another Religious named Reynolds, of the Order of St. Bridgett, being subjected to the same most cruel death, were at the same time deprived of life, one after another ; all of whose relics being thrown into cauldrons and there partially sodden, were afterwards hung up in divers places in the city. And one arm of our Father was suspended at the gate of our House, and hung there for full two days after our transmigration into Babylon. It happened, however, on the third day, that two of Ours were passing through that gate, one going from the house, the other returning, and as they stopped to meet, at the moment of meeting, that most holy arm fell to the ground, no one else seeing it, as could rarely have happened, owing to the numbers of persons passing by. Wherefore, regarding it as a miracle, we received it and placed it in a chest containing also the bloody shirt of the same our Father, in which he was martyred, and with the cause of his death written on it, by the hand of the holy William Exmew, who would have sent it to the Reverend Father then presiding in the Grande Chartreuse, if he had lived. We, however, placed the chest in a secret subterranean place, until God should bring back the Congregation and have pity on us.

It was notorious that they underwent this kind of death and punishment, and that this was the cause and occasion, and no other, is attested not only by the Acts of Parliament, but also of our holy Father himself. For after sentence of death was pronounced on him, he wrote all the questions and his answers, in this matter, with his own hand, in his writing-tablet, which tablet he sent to Father William, above mentioned, the Procurator of our House, who gave it to me, unhappy man, and I afterwards transferred it to a Spanish gentleman of probity and piety, named Peter Barin, who promised me to send the same tablet, with a portion of the shirt of our holy Father, to His Holiness the Pope, or to the Reverend Father then presiding in your House. These things, therefore, I have noted down, because some men of mean judgment say that our holy Father, with his brethren, conspired to bring about the King's death, and, therefore, justly suffered death; which is altogether false. And what need have we of witnesses? We ourselves who live, and were left behind, heard the cause from the mouth of the Lord Cromwell himself, who put it before us as often as he came, in the same form, and in the same words as I have recited above : " You shall sincerely, fully, and without any pretence, deny on oath the authority of the Pope, and of all your Superiors."

CHAPTER ELEVENTH.

OF THE EXECUTION OF THREE MORE OF THE FATHERS, AND OF THE CONTINUED AFFLICTION OF THE REMAINDER.

THOSE three Saints having been thus put to death, certain men of low condition, and not worthy to be named, came within the next three weeks to the aforesaid Vicar of the King, asking authority to make game of and maltreat other Carthusians. This request having been readily granted, they came to us in a noisy manner and carried off three other venerable Fathers, who were then our heads, namely, Father Humphrey Middlemore, then being the Vicar, and previously Procurator of our House; Father William Exmew, who had become Procurator on removal from the vicariate, and Father Sebastian Newdigate, a priest and monk of our House. These three were led off ignominiously to a most filthy prison, where for two whole months they were bound and fastened tightly with iron chains around their necks and thighs, and were cruelly made to stand erect against the posts and pillars of the house, without any relief or relaxation for any purpose whatsoever. At the end of these weeks, they were brought together before the Council and questioned on the same article on which our Father had been put to death, and the same proposals were made to them that were made to our Father, and having constantly professed that they would not go against the decrees and practices of holy mother Church, they were condemned to the same punishment, torture, and death, and within ten days, they suffered the same things as the Father.

These three were young as to age, but mature in mind, full of grace and virtues, and of illustrious family—one of whom, Father Sebastian, had been brought up in the King's house; all were especially learned and of great constancy; boldly alleging from the Sacred Scriptures, before the judges, that the King could not arrogate to himself, as of right and by Divine authority, that supremacy of the Church, which Jesus Christ our Lord gave to the Pope, and the priests.* And they went to death, as to a banquet, accepting it with the greatest meekness, and patience of heart, alacrity of body, and joyful countenance, in the hope of eternal life, the 19th of June, 1535.

From the death of these our holy Brothers, two years elapsed before others were imprisoned, but not without great tribulation to us; for a time came such as had not been from ancient days. Previously, others had fought for us, and we were silent, but now extreme necessity compelled each one of us to give an account of himself, and to stand on his own defence, all other aid being forbidden and excluded. Nor were we without conflict, nor was there one hour in the four preceding years in which we could free ourselves from tribulations; for there were either fightings without, or fears within, in expectation of what would happen.† We desired death, but it fled from us, for they sought to overcome us by tiring us out.‡ Those set over us in the House, after the seizure of our holy Vicar and his companions, were two

---

* St. Matt. xvi. 18.   † 2 Cor. vii. 5.   ‡ Apoc. ix. 6.

seculars, who treated the convent in a secular and very inhuman manner. They nurtured themselves delicately enough, but fed the convent with hunger and thirst. They took away our provisions, giving each of us a bit of cheese or some other morsel for each day's nourishment. They brought among us not Hebrews, but inebriates, not from wine, but from malice, who made sport of us, and beat us whenever they could; and others came to see what we were doing. We had, nevertheless, such confidence and boldness, that with Scripture and reason, we dared to contend against so powerful a King. Moreover, when they found that the source which supplied our aqueduct* (I speak of the constancy and fortitude of those who were not overcome), was outside the city on south (for by the sword of the spirit, which is the Word of God, and the testimony of the orthodox Doctors, the brethren defended themselves manfully, being ready to give satisfaction to all who required a reason for the faith and hope that was in them), they cut this aqueduct, making war on us. For they took away our books, which we had in our cells, that we might become unarmed, and dry with thirst.† Nevertheless, there were not far from the walls, fountains of the Saviour from which, with joy, we secretly drew life-giving water of wisdom, springing up into eternal life, of which our adversaries were unable to gainsay or deprive us. And what is not to be omitted, that though some of us were thus furnished with the shield of doctrine, yet holy innocence, and simplicity, had greater weight with most of them, and more sharply pierced the hearts of our adversaries, armed with which, those I speak of, refused to go beyond the bounds our Fathers had set them, but stood

* Judith vii. 6.   † Judith vii. 7.

their ground firmly, and confessed with their mouth as Holy Church had taught.

Furthermore, in addition to all the aforesaid evils, the King's Council left us no peace, but came to us very frequently, with threats and flatteries, in order to turn us from our purpose, and often remained with us so long in Chapter, that we were unable, owing to their long stay, to fulfil the duty of singing either Vespers or Matins,* whereby the convent suffered great weariness. Add the daily lamentation and weeping of relations and friends and others coming to see us, who endeavoured by sophistical arguments and persuasions, to separate us from the charity of Christ. Then a time of probation and trial approached, to determine to which, each man's pleasure would incline him ; to God or to the devil. Carnal liberty (which is the veritable service of the demons and of vices) was given to every one, to withdraw at his own choice, but thanks be to God, such was the holiness of life, constancy of spirit, modesty of words, cheerfulness of countenance, alacrity in deeds, and such moderation in all, as to astonish all who saw them. Although deprived of their Prior, and made orphans without a father, yet to each, his conscience was his Prior, directing him internally, and instructing him in all things. This conduct so astonished the King's Vicar, that on a certain Sunday, unwilling to be overcome by good, he ordered four of us to be taken forcibly to the Cathedral, where a great concourse of nobles and chief people were present to hear a sermon declaimed by some Reverend Father and Bishop. Our Fathers having come

---

* Public worship was carried on in the Charterhouse, without interruption, in the midst of these injuries and disturbances ; and very admirable it is that our Fathers never left off singing in choir, although so badly used, and suffering from hunger.

there, were placed in a prominent position, under the watchful eye of the sheriffs of the city, and after hearing the sermon were sent home. It matters not to write what they heard of what the pastor said, beyond this, that the sermon profited them not, not being mixed with faith.

CHAPTER TWELFTH.

OF THE SEPARATION OF THE BRETHREN WHO REMAINED CONSTANT, OF THE IMPRISONMENT AND DEATH OF TEN, AND OF THE DECEPTION PRACTISED ON THE REST TO INDUCE THEM TO SWEAR AS THE KING REQUIRED.

THE King's Council considering that all their trouble was thus likely to be wasted, and that they could in nowise pervert them, moved by a false pity, resolved to separate them from one another, by sending three of the four mentioned in the last chapter, and another who would have been the fourth on the first day, if he had not on that day happened to be priest of the week, into two other Houses of our Order in distant parts of the kingdom, on the 4th of May, 1536 (being the anniversary of the death of our holy Father in the preceding year). It was in this month, and in the ..nonth of June during four successive years, that we suffered most, though at other times we did not enjoy much peace; for in May, 1534, the first imprisonment of our Father occurred. In the same month, 1535, took place his death, and the imprisonment of our holy Father Vicar and his companions. In the third year occurred the afore-mentioned

F

dispersion of the brethren, which caused great vexation and disturbance to the whole Convent. In the fourth year, in June, took place the imprisonment of ten at once, as will appear hereafter, in which same month, in the second of these same years, the holy Father Vicar and his companions suffered. And as all the persecutions of St. Thomas of Canterbury are said to have occurred on Tuesdays, so also was the imprisonment and death of our holy Father. Moreover, the Reverend Father John, the holy Bishop of Rochester, and the Blessed Sir Thomas More, both suffered on Tuesdays; our Father with his companions, as mentioned above, the 10th Cal. July (22nd June), A.D. 1535, and Sir Thomas More the 6th of July in the same year. But let us now return to our subject.

Our four* being thus sent away and dispersed, the Council thought to lay hands on those who were deserted, who were as if they had neither walls, nor roofs, nor doors, and they came with gaping mouths to seize and disperse the flock; but God be blessed, Who gave them not as a prey to their teeth. They remained steadfast, founded upon a rock. Then they sent eight of them to a House of the Order of St. Bridgett, called Sion, distant from the city seven miles, to be persuaded by those who dwelt there to consent to the King. For there were there many famous and assuredly religious men, who bridled the boldness and constancy of our young men on this single occasion. For the Father Confessor,† the Rector of that Convent, was at the point of death at the time that our brethren were there, and calling them, he

---

* Dom Chauncey was himself one of these.

† There were there thirteen priests and four deacons, with six Lay-brothers, according to the Rule of St. Bridgett. The Rector was called Father Confessor.

said, " I beseech you, my dear Brothers, that you will give
me your forgiveness, for I am guilty, and was the cause of
the death of your Reverend Father : for I encouraged him to
undergo death for the cause for which he suffered, and for
which you are brought hither. But now I have thought
better of it, and see that it was not a fit cause for which
to suffer death." On his saying this, some of Ours, taking
into account his age and position, and also his being at the
point of death, gave credence to him. But on returning
home, conscience revived, and they refused to obey the voice
of the charmer.* Upon this, the Council, as if stung by
children's darts, became exceedingly angry, and threatened
the overthrow of the house, unless they would consent, for
during these three years, while all were of one mind, they did
not like to put any to death. A triple cord is not easily
broken.† This had been foretold by a very holy man in our
House, who died long before this time, to whom Almighty
God had revealed all we should suffer, who was wont to say :
" Be not alarmed, my brethren ; be of one mind in the House,
and in the Lord. They will never overcome you, while you
agree with one another." We now thoroughly experienced
the truth of these words.

For now the crown of our head fell. The enclosure was
divided ; one part followed Jeroboam, who made Israel to
sin : the other adhered to the house of David, mindful of the
justice of the only God, which it had learnt from its youth.
One party of the Convent, seeing how straitened they were,
the imminent danger of the overthrow of the House, that they
could gain nothing by resisting, and that all the world had
followed the King, these, overcome by weariness, committed

* Psalm lvii. 6.   † Eccles. iv. 12.

themselves to the Divine mercy, and consented to the Royal
will, yet not without great hurt to their consciences, and
many tears, and for no other reason, than that one tribe
should not be blotted out of Israel.* They took the oath, yet
saying in their hearts, whilst it was offered to them : " Thou
knowest, O Lord, how false and wicked this is, that they
force on us ; Thou knowest also what exceptions, alleviations,
and epikeias,† we have alleged and they have agreed to. Also
Thou seest the distress of the time, and that the overthrow
of the House is threatened, if we do not consent; but skin for
skin, and all that he has, a man will give for his life :‡ but
evil is not to be done that good may come ;§ Thou knowest
our hearts, and how willingly we would oppose them ; we
therefore beseech Thy clemency, that Thou wilt not regard
or accept this ceremony, which we outwardly perform, placing
our hands on the book of the holy Gospel, and kissing it, as
if we affirmed or consented to the Royal will, but wilt only
receive this our outward simulation, as a mark of veneration
for the sacred words, written down in the Gospel, in order to
preserve the House, if it shall please Thee." This is the kind
of excuse, though frivolous, which I am able to offer for those
who stumbled.   And I know for certain, that so it was done ;
but not for this, were we justified.‖   I need not recall the
history of Naaman, nor insert anything from the book of
Baruch, as persuading us to this pretence: nor will I turn
aside my heart to frame excuses for sin, knowing what is
written : " Unless your justice abound more than that of the

---

* Judges xxi, 17.
† An epikeia is a judgment that the legislator does not mean his law to bind under the circumstances.
‡ Job ii. 4.   § Romans iii. 8.   ‖ 4 Kings v. 17, 19.

Scribes and Pharisees, you shall not enter into the Kingdom of Heaven."*

The rest of the Convent knowing this full well, were not willing to regard the preservation of the House of stone, as more precious than themselves, but at once preferring the salvation of their souls to the material House, freely gave up all they had, for the sake of their salvation, and would not accept deliverance through any pretence, but with constancy opposed the King,† that they might find a better resurrection and a House not made with hands, in Heaven.‡

The number of these last was ten, three priests, Richard Bere, Thomas Johnson, and Thomas Green; one deacon, named John Davy, and six Lay-brothers, who were William Greenwood, Thomas Scryven, Robert Salt, Walter Pierson, Thomas Redyng, and William Horn, all professed of the London House. All of these, on the 4th of the calends of June, 1537, were thrust into a very foul prison in the city, called Newgate, where all (one excepted) in a short time died of the filth and foulness of the prison. The King's Vicar was greatly vexed at their deaths in this manner, swearing with a great oath that had they lived, he would have treated them more severely. The survivor, William Horn, the Lay-brother, remained safe in prison for four years. Brought forth at length to death, on the 4th of November, 1541 § he suffered as our Reverend Father, and finished his life with like cruelties. So the son followed the father, maltreated most harshly and for a long time, preferring to

---

* St. Matt. v. 20. † Hebrews xi. 35. ‡ 2 Cor. v. 1.
§ He suffered on the 4th of August, 1540. Chauncey was not in England at the time of his death.

be put to death for the love of Jesus Christ, and for the faith of His spouse, the Catholic Church, rather than to speak falsely or to perjure himself.

———

CHAPTER THIRTEENTH.

OF THE HANGING OF THE TWO REMAINING BROTHERS, AND THE FINAL DESOLATION OF THE CONVENT AND THE HOUSE.

WHILST these things were passing with us, a great tumult of the people arose in the kingdom against the King;[*] which being appeased, a certain nobleman who dwelt near the House, where two of our four expelled brethren were living, informed the King's Vicar that two of those Carthusians of the London House, whom he had sent to another House of the same Order near the town of Hull, were still rebellious, and unwilling to obey the commands of the King. On hearing this, Cromwell gave him power to deal with them according to the rigour of the law. The nobleman, in order to give effect to these much-desired commands, brought them out into the city of York, where, in the presence of the Duke of Norfolk, they gave them their measure of wheat in due season[†] (namely, the 5th of the Ides of May, 1537). They were hung in chains, until their bones fell to the ground. Their names were John Rochester and James Walworth, both of them priests and professed monks of the London House. The other two, who had been expelled with them and sent into another part of the kingdom, were, after a year and a half, sent by the Visitors of the Order, appointed by

* Called the Pilgrimage of Grace.   † St. Luke xii. 42.

the King's Vicar, to the above-mentioned House of the Order
of St. Bridgett, where, after some debate, they fell at length
into that method of simulation (by some called epikeia) into
which the others had fallen, and yielded to the King's will, in
reliance on a certain fallacious hope, and allured, drawn away,
and seduced by empty persuasions and promises, of the com-
plete and lasting stability and preservation of the House on
our consenting to the Royal will. But no other House was
more speedily ruined.

For, within a year after we had thus consented, they
cancelled their bargain. We were all expelled from the
house and led into Babylon, to the number of twelve professed monks, three guests, and six professed Lay-brothers.
This was done on the 15th of November, 1538, a day very
bitter, on which our inheritance was given over to others, our
House to strangers, and converted to the vilest uses. In the
church, they placed tents and implements of war, they hewed
with axes, not only the images of the saints, but even of the
Crucified, and stamped upon them. They leapt on the holy
altars, danced, and played with dice, and committed in that
sacred place other detestable and abominable things, rather
to be wept over than related. But in the year before last,
our House, cleansed from this filth, was given to a certain
Sir Edward* North, who built himself a palace there, and
made a banqueting-hall of the church, and almost entirely
overthrew the cloister.

This, Reverend Father, is the end of my report, and that
was the sleep which God gave to your sons, His beloved ones,
because fruit is to the just. So God judged them in the
earth, to bring forth more fruit in patience, and to acquire

* The house given to Sir Edward North (36 Hen. VIII. 1544).

greater glory in the inheritance of the Lord, which, we cannot
doubt, God gives to His Saints (for whom all things work
together for good), who have never swerved from their faith
in Him.

CHAPTER FOURTEENTH.

OF THE REVELATIONS BY WHICH THE LORD GLORIFIED HIS MARTYRS AFTER THEIR DEATH.

PASSING over the law and the testimony, as well as the
internal conviction and witness of the spirit, which some of
Ours have had concerning the life and glory of our holy
martyrs ; I will relate in a few words, a certain miracle, and
then a vision, and another revelation, in order that their seed
may be known by the Gentiles, and their budding in the
midst of the people, that all who see and hear, may know
these are the seed whom God hath blessed.

There was a certain Brother named Richard Crofts, in the
House of St. Anne of our Order, near the city of Coventry,
who shortly after the death of our Father and our aforesaid
brethren, being greatly oppressed by various temptations, fell
into the snare of the devil, despairing of the mercy of God,
and purposed to drown himself in a pond in the garden of the
Convent. To accomplish this, he left his cell, in the silence
of night, at about nine o'clock, and coming to the place he
had thought of, he tried to cast himself in, but could not, and
walking up and down the bank until eleven o'clock, he tried
several times to accomplish his wicked intention, but was
always prevented. Being absent on the assembling of the

Convent for Matins, the Infirmarian going to his cell, and not finding him, informed the Prior, who went with others to the absent man's cell, and seeing there a ladder against the wall, suspected he had taken flight. Then one of them, by a sudden inspiration, going up the ladder, looked into the convent garden, and behold he saw around the pond, a great light, and calling the Prior and the others, they all ran there in haste. Having entered the garden, they saw the Brother walking on one side of the pond, trying repeatedly to drown himself, yet always prevented, and they (not all, but two only) saw the great light on the other side, and in it, as they affirmed, they saw all our Fathers who had suffered, interposing themselves between the Brother and the water, as often as he tried to drown himself. But when they approached the bank of the pond, the light disappeared, and having arrested the Brother, who was trembling and almost speechless, they led him to his cell, where, on a fire being lighted, and his spirit revived, they asked what he had intended to do. He replied that he went there to drown himself, in order to get more quickly out of this mortal life, as he knew he was to be damned, but, said he, " I was not able, for I was held back by some who prevented me, and interposed themselves between me and the water, but I saw no one, nor do I know who they were." The Reverend Father of that Convent, who was present on the occasion, communicated what had occurred to some in our House, adding that the Brother was at once freed from his dreadful temptation.

Now I come to a revelation. There were two monks in our Convent of London, closely united in pious and familiar affection. It happened that one of them, named Robert Raby, shortly after the death of our Reverend Father, took to his bed through illness, where after a time he died. The other, being his great friend, went to visit him, and among other things, said to the sick man, "Dear Brother, you are going the way of all flesh. I earnestly beg of you that when it shall be well with you, you will return, if God will permit, and tell me what has happened to our Fathers, and in what state they are." The other replied he would do as he was asked, if it were the will of Heaven. One week afterwards, the sick man was laid with his fathers, and when the fifth day after his death had come, the other Brother, who was alive and well, walked in his cell at about four o'clock in the morning, in prayer and meditation. Suddenly the Brother who was dead appeared to him in white raiment, and took a turn with him in his cell. Being asked who he was, he replied, "Your Brother, who on such a day migrated out of this life," and being asked how it was with him and with our Fathers, answered, "It is well with me. I am in heavenly glory, and thanks be to God, am enjoying the glorious vision of God, but I am in a much less and lower glory than our Fathers who suffered, for they are in great glory crowned with the palm of martyrdom, and our Father Prior has a crown more splendid than the rest." Having said this, he disappeared.

This vision being afterwards related to the King's Council, the Brother to whom it was related was summoned, and after many inquiries and examinations, warned with threats not to disclose it;* but I relate it to your Paternity, in order to make you more sure of the glory of their reward in the inheritance of the Lord, although it may be better

---

* This account is in the British Museum, written and signed by Darley himself (Cod. MS. Cotton).

known by the law and the testimony, since they suffered for truth and justice, to which the Kingdom of Heaven is due, according to the Divine promise;* of which promise, I am unfit to speak, since I am unjust and left it; and certainly, if I could be ashamed, and if my heart were not depraved, and malignant, and even diabolical, it would be more fitting for me, on account of grief and confusion to weep, than to write, considering where I am, and where I am not, what I have, and what I have lost, where I am going, and from what I am shut out. But I beseech your Holiness to have pity on my misery, and aid me before the Highest with your holy prayers,† lest the Lord should be ashamed of me, when He shall come in His Majesty before God and His angels, Whom I have oftentimes been ashamed of and dishonoured by my unrighteous deeds, and give me a place of habitation in the House (of Val de Grace), (at the instance of whose Reverend Prior and his devout Convent, I have taken on myself the task of writing this history), where I will hide my head, and cover with perfect penance, the young which my misery hath begotten to me, in the land of my captivity, and may by the grace of God recover the years which the locust consumed in my iniquity and malice;‡ I ask the same also for a devout Brother named John Perdon, who journeyed together with me into a foreign land, having been a guest in our House at London, at the time of its dissolution; and for a Lay-brother named Hugh Taylor,§ professed in our House, who came here with me. And that you will be pleased, with kind and

---

* St. Matt. v. 10. † St. Luke ix. 26. ‡ Joel ii. 25.

§ He alone came with Dom M. Chauncey, the other later. He is the Brother whose testimony is given for some wonderful things that happened in the London House, and to whom it is said the beautiful vision was vouchsafed which is mentioned in chapter 2.

serene countenance, and goodwill, to accept this unpolished
and rude work, not as from one offering gold or silver or
precious stones, but as from "a young calf that bringeth forth
horns and hoofs." And may the sweet and merciful Jesus
Christ our Lord keep your Reverend Paternity, with all
yours, safe to eternal life. Farewell. Amen.

EPILOGUE.

IN these things, which I have commemorated concerning these holy martyrs, I have traced out only the leading points. For it seemed best and less tedious, both to myself and the reader, instead of burthening the narrative with rambling stories and commentaries, to relate in detail, those things of which I had personal knowledge and experience, or in which I took a considerable part : but I have thought that by way of appendix I might add, that none of those who brought about the dissolution, long outlived the work, or received any lasting pleasure from their evil deeds ; since, not long afterwards, all perished by a violent and ignominious death, or came to great poverty, or fell into the worst calamities of human life ; even Thomas Cromwell, the King's Vicar, within two years of our overthrow, lost his head for high treason. The Guardians of our House, falling into poverty and mendicity, finished their lives miserably ; a woman, who, in contempt of the Church, entered our House whilst we were engaged in sacred functions, expired unhappily, that is, in the greatest agony, within the fifth day afterwards.

Therefore, it is true, what the Psalmist says, " Precious in the sight of the Lord is the death of His saints,"* which is the end of their labours, the consummation of victory, and the entrance to eternal life ; so, on the other hand, very bad is the death of the wicked, whose birth also is evil, and their life and

* Psalm cxv. 15.

destiny much worse than that of the holy martyrs, who were
ordained to heavenly glory, after the lapse of this space of
painful warfare.   But to the deserts of the others, God as a
just Judge has destined eternal punishments in the burning
abyss of Hell, from which may our Lord Jesus Christ, our
only Saviour, mercifully defend you.   Amen.

www.ingramcontent.com/pod-product-compliance
Lightning Source LLC
Chambersburg PA
CBHW022014050726
47499CB00007BA/2580